# Open Me First

*A Revelation Cove Valentine's Day novella*

## ELIZA GORDON

**SGA**
BOOKS

Cover and interior design by SGA Books
Valentine's Day Envelope image by InspirationGP
Chapter header image by Anna Ivonina

E-book ISBN-13: 978-1-989908-59-4
Paperback ISBN-13: 978-1-989908-60-0

www.sgabooks.com | www.elizagordon.com

# Also by Eliza Gordon

# About the Author

A native of Portland, Oregon, Eliza Gordon (a.k.a. Jennifer Sommersby) has always lived along the West Coast. Since 2002, home has been a suburb of Vancouver, British Columbia. When not lost in a writing project, she works as a freelance editor (via Plumfield Editing), mom, wife, bibliophile, Superman freak, and humble servant to three pampered tuxedo cats (@tuxietrionurojo on Instagram).

Eliza writes women's fiction, romantic comedy, and enviromance; Jennifer Sommersby writes young adult fiction. Both personalities are represented by Stacey Kondla at The Rights Factory.

Want to buy direct from Eliza? Visit the SGA Books Shopify store!

*Authors, find and nurture bookish friends like Deb and Katrin and Katie and LJ, strong, damn funny women who provide much-needed comic relief and subplots AND give you the kick in the pants to believe you can do hard things.*

# Land Acknowledgment

I would like to acknowledge that I live and work on the traditional, ancestral, and unceded territory of the **Coast Salish**, **Kwikwetlem**, **Tsleil-Waututh**, **S'ólh Téméxw (Stó:lō)**, and **Qayqayt** people. I am grateful for the privilege of living in this beautiful place.

# 1

Chef Joseph is trying very hard not to lose his patience. I warned him cookie decorating would not be a skill in my wheelhouse, that I don't understand how to *flood* my icing without it running over the sides and onto the parchment paper. When he demonstrates *wet-on-wet* technique, everyone at the stainless steel prep table gets it to work for their heart- and flower-shaped sugar cookies except me, and then Tabby starts making crude jokes about *wet on wet*, followed by another line of inappropriate banter when Chef encourages us to use the *luster dust* on our creations, only Tabby misheard him and thought he said *lusty dust*, and yeah . . .

Poor Chef. I would be frustrated too. Last I checked, teaching cookie decorating to grown toddlers was not in his job description.

But we have two Valentine's Day events in the next ten days, so he recruited help to make a bazillion cookies and I got caught in the dragnet when Miss Betty lured me into the kitchen with a plate of fresh brownies. She held it right under my nose and *mmm*, so fragrant and delicious, I had no choice but to put down my pen and follow her from the back office into the kitchen where the door was locked behind me, precluding any opportunity for escape.

*Paint cookies or no brownies*, my mother-in-law said. So mean.

Alas, here I am. The upside: I get to eat the cookies I screw up. The downside: My eyeballs are doing the Glucose Boogie in their sockets.

Midsession, my phone rings, and all the luster from floods of royal icing disappears because it's Nils, Ryan's assistant coach, calling me at 2:30 p.m. on a workday, and I'm pretty sure he's not after a recipe.

"Hey, Hollie. Don't freak out."

My heart thuds. "That is a shit way to start a phone call, Nils. Where's Ryan? Wait—is that a siren?"

"Sorry. You're right. Um, he's fine. I mean, mostly fine. Other than the bone sticking from his arm, and he probably has a concussion, but yeah, you know how tough he is."

"What is going on?" I don't mean to yell. It startles the sous-chef next to me and she screws up the intricate floral design she's spent the last ten minutes piping.

"In practice, a couple guys got a bit aggressive and lost track of their positioning and Coach just happened to be in their way, so boom!"

"Boom? That's it? Nils, did you mention a bone? Let me talk to Ryan."

"Hang on—the paramedic is poking him with a needle for an IV and pain medicine."

The kitchen has stopped moving, everyone's widened eyes on me. Miss Betty is immediately by my side. Yeah, sure, I'm worried, but Ryan is her *child*. I rest my free hand on her forearm in reassurance.

"Here you go, Hollie, here he is."

Shuffling, followed by, "Hey, babe."

"Ryan, what the fuck? Are you OK? Is there really a bone sticking out of your arm? Oh my god, which arm is it?"

"The left."

Shit, that's his cougar arm.

"But the nice man in the dark blue coat just gave me morphine, so can I call you back when we get to the hospital and I know more?" I hear the pain in his voice, morphine or not. "Hols, don't

2

worry. I'll be OK. I don't need you to swoop in and save me this time."

"The hell you don't."

He snorts. "Hollie, I swear, I will call you when I talk to a doctor. Everything'll be fine. It always works out, doesn't it?"

Miss Betty leans close and talks into the phone's speaker end. "Hi, Ryan, it's Mom. I love you. We all love you." Her voice cracks.

"Babe, tell my mother I'm fine and I'll call you guys back. Love you too."

*Beep beep beep.*

The eight or so cookie decorators stare back at me, the kitchen silent other than the soft whirr of the ventilation hood. I pick up another messed-up heart and bite into it. Chef shuffles over to the walk-in and pulls out cold butter to make another batch of dough.

⇜

An hour later, my brother-in-law Tanner, Miss Betty, Tabby, and I are in the apartment I share with Ryan. I'm pacing a path in the area rug while Miss Betty tidies, because that's what she does when she's anxious, and I am embarrassed but also relieved that there's enough disarray in here to keep her occupied. Tanner has a DVR'd hockey game muted on the TV, though he's hunched over his phone, no doubt updating Sarah, his wife, while Tabby, the dear, makes tea and coffee and throws together a quick chicken salad to counteract all the sugar I've consumed today.

I call my dad and update him with as much as I know. He says he's packing a bag and is on his way and will meet us in Vancouver. It's about a five-hour drive from Portland to the truck crossing in Blaine, Washington, longer if Seattle traffic sucks or with heavy border lineups. I try to insist that Nurse Bob stay home until we know more, but he refuses, says he'd rather come on up now instead of waiting for his planned trip next month "because someone's gotta make sure that boy listens to the medical professionals."

That's my dad.

Finally, an ER doctor who sounds like a fifth grader calls to double-check medication allergies before Ryan's taken into surgery. Dr. Puberty also provides a more detailed account of events: Ryan was on the ice, near the boards, overseeing a drill when several players collided and piled into him, which wouldn't have been that big of a deal if he hadn't impacted the ice with his *and* their body weight on the arm Chloe the Cougar mangled, the one Ryan has had multiple surgeries on to reconstruct and months of physiotherapy to regain use and functional strength.

But he landed hard on that patchwork appendage and snapped the humerus with enough vigor that it punctured the skin, making it a compound fracture—*and* he smacked his head on the wall as he tumbled, splitting open his eyebrow, and then bounced his un-helmeted noggin off the ice, so he definitely has a concussion. Ryan Fielding never does anything half-assed.

"How long will he be in surgery? I'm about three hours away, maybe more. You're in Langley?"

"Yes, Langley Memorial. I'm not sure when your husband will be going in or how long it'll take—I do know, however, that it'll be a complicated repair. I can have the orthopedic surgeon call you before they get underway, if you'd prefer?"

"Yes, please. Thank you." I rattle off Tanner's and Miss Betty's numbers as backup before Dr. Puberty hangs up. "Who's up for a trip to the big city?"

# 2

Tanner is our primary pilot, and a floatplane is the fastest way to get from this rocky outcropping to the bigger rocky outcropping known as Vancouver. So he packs a change of clothes from the stash he keeps in his mom's apartment here at the lodge and then smooches Sarah and little Elsbeth farewell and barters that he will bring home Els's favorite person in the world if she will just let go of his leg.

The plan: We'll fly into Vancouver Harbour and then take a Lyft to the hospital in Langley. It is my sincerest hope that by the time we arrive at our destination, I will have received word from the surgeon that Ryan's bone is tucked back inside the fleshy bits, zipped up where it belongs, and that my best friend with benefits is in recovery, sleeping off the anesthesia.

Until then, however, I shall bring my iPad so in flight, I can clean up my inboxes, a tedious, loathsome task but a great distraction. And since I am already tearing holes in my cuticles (a habit I cannot break despite Tabby's efforts to beautify my fingers with sparkly gel polish that I peel off within an hour of application), sorting through email will give me something benign to focus on and thus settle the Chicken Little voice in my head yelling about surgery complications and/or floatplane engine failure.

Before we even lift off the surface of the Salish Sea, I'm fretting about how much Ryan will fight me about coming home to the resort for postop R&R. He'll want to recuperate at our Langley apartment so he can report to the arena every day and carry on his duties as the head coach of the Giants, a major junior hockey club. Admirable? Sure.

But I know Ryan too well. If he stays on the mainland, he'll refuse to take it easy because he loves his job, he loves his players and his coaching staff—he won't want to do anything to disappoint them, especially since the team is at the top of the standings as we near the second week of February. They are gunning for a playoff spot, and losing their head coach weeks before the end of the season was definitely not on management's agenda.

And yet, my husband losing use of his arm or suffering lasting problems from the concussion because he's not properly rehabilitated is not on *my* agenda. Five-plus years in, we're still technically newlyweds; I, Hollie Porter Fielding, have *needs*, and my husband is the only man I want servicing those needs for the rest of my life.

As such, I will invoke the "in sickness and in health" clause and demand he come home to the Cove for a couple weeks where he shall allow us to dote on him for a change. Ryan does everything for everyone.

Not on my watch, sir. Not this time.

Plus, with Nurse Bob on the job, Ryan won't have any choice but to comply. It'll be nice to have the old man around for a bit. I miss him like crazy.

Am I happy my better half was injured to the point of requiring general anesthesia and scalpels and probably even more hardware that will trigger metal detectors at airports?

Absolutely not.

Am I sad he will be with me over the next ten-plus days and that Valentine's Day is next Thursday so I will be able to make him forget about his sore arm and brain for a few hours via my naked feminine wiles and a generous sprinkling of lusty dust?

It's almost like I'm an evil cookie genius or something.

# 3

Ryan's surgery was long—he was still in the OR when our hired car pulled curbside in the hospital turnaround—but it was a success, thank all the deities. They opted to keep him overnight with the tentative promise they'll discharge him today, depending on the head CT, for which we are awaiting his turn. The neurologist is confident Ryan has a grade 2 concussion, but the doc wants to make sure there's nothing more sinister going on underneath the cranial eggshell.

My dad arrived last night right as my groggy husband was rousing (and ralphing) from the anesthesia, and though I tried to keep my shit together, I melted into tears when Dad, bathed in heavenly light, strolled into the room. Can't help it—I will always be a daddy's girl. When my father is around, I can relax for a second, let him be the adult. And he speaks fluent Doctor, so when is that not helpful?

I am beyond grateful he dropped everything to hurry north. Dad and Ryan are thick as thieves, so in the coming days when Nurse Bob explains to my beloved former concierge why he can't go play hockey coach with his friends, Ryan will listen. Dad will diligently check the bandaging and positioning of the busted arm, plus he can eventually pluck out the eyebrow sutures so I don't have to. *Ewwww.*

Midday, the neurologist returns with news that nothing freaky is happening in Ryan's gray matter. However, with his assessment, he delivers the stinging blow: "No stress, no yelling, no ice time, no overthinking, no meetings, very limited screentime ..." The list includes more than this, but Ryan has long tuned out by the time the short bald guy in the white lab coat and expensive loafers shuffles from the hospital room.

When the orthopedic surgeon comes in to recheck and sign off on discharge, she basically reiterates everything the brain guy just said about taking time off work and resting as much as possible. My darling husband actually sighs and flops his head into his pillow upon hearing this proclamation for a second time in under an hour.

Like I said, good damn thing Nurse Bob is here.

Truth be told, this isn't Ryan's first or even third concussion. The arm will heal as well as it can, given the former Chloe-delivered trauma that will certainly mess with recovery. But smacking his brain against its case, a brain that has a history of smacks throughout a prolonged hockey career—yeah, Ryan needs quiet time. Even if he doesn't like it.

"I guess I'm the boss for a few days," I say, gently removing a flake of dried blood from his forehead. Whoever sutured his eyebrow did a fantastic job.

"When are you not the boss?"

I plant a gentle kiss on his lips. "Good boy."

# 4

With enough medication on board to make it look like we tipped over a pharmacy, we're at last en route back to Revelation Cove. Tanner's piloting, talking via the headsets with my dad while I make sure Ryan is as padded as we could get him in the airplane seat.

Knowing he'd need extra comfort, Tanner and I flew down in the air taxi we use almost exclusively for guest transport. Couple years ago, we added a second plane to our tiny fleet—more guests means more trips back and forth—and Miss Lily is *not* a bird I would offer to paying guests, even with the duffel bag of travel-size liquor bottles Ryan keeps tucked behind the front seats.

"How are you feeling? Can I get you anything?" I ask.

My gorgeous husband rolls his head against the headrest. "Stop. Asking. Me."

"Babe, I just want to make sure you're all right. I know you won't complain, so I have to ask a thousand times."

"If I promise to complain, will you stop hovering?"

I lean across the armrest that divides our seats and smooch his bearded cheek. "I will never stop hovering. You are my love god."

His grin lights a nuclear reactor in my chest. I shall never tire of it.

"Hols, I promise I will let you know if I need something."

The plane shudders; I clamp down on Ryan's thigh. Maybe I should sort some more emails. I only got halfway through my Promotions tab.

"Sorry," Tanner says. "All good. Everything's fine."

I look ahead through the windshield, then through the porthole-size window on my left. The sky is a rich blue, no clouds, a fantastic February day. We had a vicious storm at Christmas and pissy weather lingered into the first couple weeks of January, but since, it's been like spring can't wait to bust free.

Another wind buffets into our flying tin can.

"Tanner . . ." I lean forward and poke his shoulder.

"We're fine. Just a bit breezy in through here."

Ryan taps my foot with his. "Babe, tell me what I've missed. What are you working on these days?"

He knows how much I don't like the floatplane, how I will always choose the boat if offered the choice, no matter how much longer water travel takes or how many statistics he shares about how safe air travel is *blah blah blah*.

"Um, so, I just started a course on how to improve SEO and ads campaign strategies for the website. I signed up for a series of beginner illustration classes so I can learn to use the Wacom pad thing Dad got me for Christmas—"

"Have you drawn me any otters yet?" Dad asks from the front.

"I've drawn blobs that might be otters someday," I say. My dad insists that learning to draw will stave off Alzheimer's (no idea why this is relevant to me at thirty), so he bought me a tablet and digital pencil, and honestly, I'm too embarrassed to admit that wee Elsbeth draws better than I do.

Of course Elsbeth is a prodigy. I delivered her.

Another wind knocks into us.

"Fucking hell," I whisper, squeezing my eyes closed. I do *not* want to crash into this tentacle of the Pacific Ocean today.

Ryan wraps his good hand around my fingers clenched on his

thigh. "Speaking of Elsbeth, what's she been up to? Has she stopped talking about the raccoons yet?"

"Only because you sent her the stuffed one."

With the next bump of turbulence, my dad's phone slides between the seat and the center console onto the carpeted floor. I wait until we've for sure evened out before I reach for it to hand back to him.

As I lift it, the screen awakens and reveals a text message preview.

> Can't wait to see you again, Bobby. Thanks for the other night. 🩶

The sender's name—Lady Marmalade—has a cheesy heart in place of an actual profile picture.

*Oh my god. (A), my dad has a girlfriend, and (b), she likes* Moulin Rouge?

I thought he hated musicals.

Why hasn't he told me he's met someone? Who is she? How long has he been seeing her? Is she someone from work?

And what the hell did they do the other night?

"Hol?" Ryan squeezes my hand. "You OK?"

"What? Yeah." I slide free of Ryan's grasp to scoot forward in my seat. "Dad—" He's talking away. I tap his shoulder with his phone, the screen again dark. "You dropped this." I point toward the floor behind his seat. I don't think he hears me over the conversation in his headset, but he nods and mouths *thank you.*

I sit back and refasten my belt, leaning over to whisper in Ryan's ear.

"I saw something I probably wasn't supposed to see."

He hikes an eyebrow in question.

"My dad—he's got some action going on."

Ryan smirks.

"Gross! It's my *dad.*"

"He's still human, babe. And he's healthy and—"

"Do *not* say virile or I will punch your bad arm."

"Ohhh, too soon, Hols."

I rest my lips right against his ear. "It's OK for me to do unholy things to your body, but I do NOT want to think about my dad and—"

Yet another bubble of turbulence rattles our cage, and I grab Ryan's cast-wrapped arm. He winces.

"Sorry! Sorry!" I lift my hands away from his person.

"It's fine . . . I'm good."

I heave forward and dig into the pocket on the back of the pilot's seat, beyond grateful to find a tiny dram of Bulleit Bourbon. I crack the lid and pour the burning amber ounce down my gullet, praying that Tanner gets this aircraft under control because I do *not* want my last thoughts in this world to be about my father having sex with some frisky coworker.

Oh my god, it's like Len and Troll Lady in the wheelchair-accessible bathroom all over again.

And lord knows a hospital is *filled* with wheelchair-accessible bathrooms.

# 5

W e land. Safely. We do not die.
Tanner helps his brother from the plane and then
along and up the dock to the main pathway that leads to the grand
front doors. My dad and I follow, him *tsking* at me all the way
about chugging two of the tiny bottles, reminding me that Lucy
Collins, my biological mother, is an alcoholic and thus I am
genetically susceptible to favoring the drink and "You are too old
to be day-drinking, especially when your husband is in such rough
shape."

I don't have the heart to tell him that I needed to sterilize my
brain from seeing that text message, from envisioning whatever
*Grey's Anatomy* scene he's been reenacting with Lady Marmalade.

"Dad, I hate flying and then landing on *water*. You know that."

"Mm-hmm."

I haven't had enough to eat today, so that bourbon went right to
my head. I stub my toe on a paver, and the heavy bag over my
shoulder full of Ryan's medical supplies tumbles forward, though I
don't drop it.

"Are you seriously drunk, young lady?"

"DAD, I'm fine. This bag is heavy."

14

He leans in and sniffs at me. I stop walking. "If you're going to be a jerk, I will have Tanner fly you back to Portland."

He snorts and keeps going up the slight incline. "You wish."

"Helloooooooo! My baby boy is home!" Our spat is summarily squashed when Miss Betty hurries out the front door, her arms aloft as she approaches her sons. She's careful about hugging Ryan, though he leans to kiss her cheek.

"Daddyyyyyyy!" In Betty's wake, Elsbeth flies out the front door, clomping toward us in her favorite rain boots. (They're printed with sea otters. I bought them for her. Because I'm basically the most awesome auntie in the whole world.) Els throws her arms around Tanner's legs right as Dad and I catch up.

"Auntie and Grampa Bob! Are we having a party?" Elsbeth launches herself toward my dad; he drops his overnight bag and scoops her up. She gives him a tight hug, but when she turns around, preparing to hop into Ryan's embrace, she freezes.

"Unca, what *happened*?" She stares at Ryan's bandaged arm, the bruise and sutured cut above his left eyebrow. "Did you get in another fight with a cougar?"

"Something like that, kiddo."

"You really gotta be more careful," she says, pointing a scolding finger at him.

"That's what I told him too," I say.

Elsbeth leans toward me, indicating it's Auntie's turn, even though she's growing so fast, by dinner, she might be ready to borrow my clothes. Only she'll flip through my closet and tell me I have terrible fashion sense and declare that she'd rather wear Gramma Betty's hand-me-downs.

She wraps me in a tight hug and announces, "Hollie Cat, Acorn pooped by the fireplace, but I smelled it before the Roomba drove through it again." Then she wiggles free, giggling like mad when one of her rain boots slips off in the process. "Unca, when can you skate with me? I've been practicing."

Els gently takes Ryan's good hand and walks with him into the lodge, talking the whole time about what she's been up to in the weeks since he was last home. The last third of Ryan's coaching season is always hectic, especially when they're doing so well. What am I saying . . . the beginning of the season is hectic, too, as new players acclimate and the coaches figure out who fits where.

It's a lot of hectic, and even when he's here, he's not always *here*.

He loves what he does. Coaching has reinvigorated him. I would never ask him to give it up.

But I miss the shit out of him when we're apart.

At Christmas, we talked about me maybe relocating to the mainland, maybe look for some new adventures there. We both know my job is flexible—I can maintain the resort's website and social media accounts and advertising campaigns and newsletters and all that from anywhere I have an internet connection. Ryan agreed. Seemed excited, even.

But then he went back to Langley, his guys were playing great hockey, and the conversation stalled.

Perhaps while he's convalescing, we can revisit. Firm up our plans. Talk about things like fixed vs. variable rate mortgages and built-in bookshelves and the kind of bathtub where you can fit two *and* submerge all the important parts at the same time. And I'm not averse to sliding into one of my most recent Valentine's Day-themed acquisitions to hasten negotiations. Does it matter if it's barely enough lace to cover my belly button?

I am nothing if not a master debater.

# 6

As much as everyone wants to say hello and see how Ryan's doing, he's exhausted. I record a quick video of us in our small kitchen, waving and sharing that "Ryan will catch up with everyone over the next few days" and then send it via the resort's private group chat. That should keep the wolves at bay. I mean, yeah, there are worse problems to have than staff who love their fearless leader.

It's so cheesy and almost red flaggy to say "we're a family operation," but we kind of are. Not like everyone is related, but it's a close-knit group. If you're a dick, you don't last long. We get those every once in a while, someone who blows in and thinks they're gonna take charge or be the funny fun guy who complains about having to work when they thought they were getting a paid summer vacation at an exclusive resort owned by famous ex-NHL'ers. They don't usually collect more than a single pay period's wages.

It's a good group. Sometimes I pinch myself to make sure it's all real, that Ryan is my husband, that I get to live this life.

All because my dad bought me a sweethearts spa & stay gift certificate all those years ago that I treated my newly single self to.

I kind of have the world's best dad, if I hadn't mentioned it yet today.

Need more proof? He's elbow-deep in the bag of drugs and gauze on the kitchen island, sorting and organizing the loot, stowing antibiotics in the fridge, and counting out pain meds into a rectangular pill sorter old people use to remember their daily multivitamins and heart medication. I won't tease my husband that he requires a pill sorter because as soon as I do, a fresh calamity will befall me and we will have to sleep with the pill sorter on its own cushion between us so we can take turns swallowing assorted analgesia.

"Hollie, let's get him set up in the bedroom—"

"Nah, it's too early for bed. I can hang out with you guys."

My dad ignores my husband and points me toward the bedroom. "Pillows, lots of pillows. You have a TV in there?" Nurse Bob then fills two Blender Bottles, one with fresh water, the other with Ryan's trusty green vitamin drink (*shudder*) and counts out the next dose of medication. He even has a chart in a folder to keep track of everything. Awwww . . .

I've stacked all the pillows against the headboard, cracked the window, and dragged the nightstand closer so Ryan has access to the remote, his beverages, the charging port for his phone. I open the nightstand drawer to see if there's a box of tissue—

Nope. Just a collection of multicolored vibrators and assorted bottles of lube, some flavored, some empty, and the red faux-fur handcuffs (wedding present) that Ryan rather fancies.

*Do I have time to gather all this and dump it in my dresser? What if Dad opens it?*

"Hollie, tell my father-in-law I'm fine to sit out here," Ryan protests as he shuffles into our bedroom.

"She can't help you. I bartered your release from the hospital contingent upon my promise that you'd get decent rest." Dad is right on Ryan's heels.

*Shit.*

I close the drawer of debauchery.

"Hollie, climb over from the other side and set up the pillows for that arm."

I follow orders and run around our king-size bed, careful not to jostle too much with my pillow arrangement as Ryan relents, sits, and allows my dad to remove his shoes, complaining about how he is not an invalid and this is ridiculous and we're making a big deal out of nothing.

I can't take my eyes off the nightstand.

Dad's got Ryan's shoes off, the two men still nattering at each other as Dad lifts my husband's legs one at a time onto the mattress, and then assists as Ryan melts against the plush landing pad of fiberfill and feathers. And as if on cue, Ryan sneezes, the action followed by a quick moan from the pain rippling through his body.

"Kleenex!" he says, cupping his good hand over his slightly crooked nose.

And in perfectly timed response, my dad, noting there is no tissue box on top of the nightstand, proceeds to open the drawer, eyes widening in slow motion as he stares at and registers the contents, closes the drawer, looks at his son-in-law whose hand is still cupped around his nasal cannon, and then to me. A smirk tugs at his lips as he pivots into the en suite and grabs the tissue off the back of the toilet.

"Not a word," I utter as Dad hands over the flower-printed box.

"I wouldn't dream of it." He swallows his laugh on a hiccup.

# 7

Because Valentine's Day is next Thursday, a workday, we took advantage and scheduled *two* weekends of posh pampering for lovebirds looking to get away—this weekend before and then next weekend closer to the actual Hallmark holiday. Hey, if people want to spend their hard-earned cash to come up here to drink our booze and gorge on Chef Joseph's culinary cunnilingus, I will gladly swipe their credit cards and hand over the goodie bag of sheet-sullying party favors.

Side note: I ordered extra gloves, surgical masks, and OxiClean for the housekeeping team. It maybe be Cupid's big day, but last time I checked, he's not keen on postcoital clean-up.

Rude little freak.

My dad has been gracious enough to only wink and waggle his eyebrows a couple times since discovering the treasure in our nightstand. When he's not following Ryan around with an extra pillow or a little white cup of drugs, he's outside playing with Elsbeth and Acorn or laughing it up astride a stool as Miss Betty bakes her heart out for the incoming king tide of horny houseguests.

I *love* having my dad here.

Even when I catch him giggling like a teenager in one of the wingback chairs near the massive fireplace, his phone cupped in his hand, thumbs flying across the screen. I consider interrupting, ask what's got him so giddy—but then I remember the text from Lady Marmalade and flash a smile and the *I love you* sign and divert into the back office in search of something to keep my mind off my dad doing *that.*

*Jeez, grow up, Hollie.*

*Fine.* Let's think about YOUR dad having sexy funtime.

Awkward, right?

Your honor, no further questions.

By dinner, the last of our expected guests have checked in, the dining room and lounge are hopping, and poor Tanner is dragging himself through the lobby, exhausted from three back-and-forth trips from Victoria and Vancouver to our island. For those who opted to take the watercraft shuttle to Revelation Cove, we have two certified sailors who've been taking turns with the runs from the mainland and Victoria Harbour, so at least they're getting a break in between.

But Tanner is the only pilot right now. When Ryan was still here full time, he and Tanner split the piloting duties. I'm worried we may need to bring on another full-time air jockey if business stays as brisk as it has been.

Again, these are good problems.

Once my portion of the day's duties are handled, I sneak into the kitchen and build a tray of food for my sweet husband who has *mostly* followed Nurse Bob's orders and slept as much as possible, other than when Dad has had Ryan on his feet, walking twice a day around the property, only possible because February continues to behave like May. If there were snow on the ground, no way we'd risk slippery steps or pathways.

Ryan is a tough guy—most hockey players are—so a broken humerus, now surgically repaired, is no big deal. I'm more worried about the headaches. He never whines, but he gets this twitch in his left eyelid when he's in pain. And his eyes are a bit droopy—Dad says it's just from the pain meds and the antibiotics wreaking havoc on his gut. "Rest, Hollie. That's what he needs. You have to convince him to slow down. Maybe take another few weeks before going back."

Yeah, that won't happen. Ryan's been on the phone with Nils and his coaching staff whenever he's not sleeping. They're live-streaming practice for his input. And he's watching game video, even though it's obviously aggravating his headaches.

But now it's Friday night, his team is at an away game in Saskatoon under the care and handling of Nils et al., and we have a resort full of amorous drunks. I will feed my man and do what I can to bring him comfort.

Starting with a proper bath.

Ryan emerges from our bedroom, his phone on speaker and held in front of his mouth, discussing switching up lines and reminding the defensemen of their positional play and aggressive forechecking. After all this time, I should be able to translate most of what he and Nils talk about—some I can, but mostly I turn it all into sexual innuendo because inside, I'm a prepubescent pervert.

"Hollie's here," Ryan says, leaning over for a kiss. He looks delicious in his gray sweatpants and robe draped around his naked torso.

"Hi, Hollie."

"Hey, Nils. Thanks for looking after things."

"Take care of our boy so we can get him back soon."

"Oh, I plan on it." I wink at Ryan and move past to let him finish his call. Even though we live at the resort, I only ask housekeeping to help me deep-clean once every couple months, not because I'm incapable but because I'm busy. Also, when Ryan isn't home, I am not proud of how I let things go.

Our tub is pristine, thanks to the diligent efforts of Elsie, one of my favorite staffers. (I'm not supposed to have favorites. Obviously I do.)

I open the bathtub tap, letting it run a little hot just in case Nils keeps Ryan on the phone and the water cools. While the tub fills, I grab a clear plastic recycling bag that I will wrap around Ryan's bandaged arm and shoulder to prevent it from taking on water. Because as smexy as he is in those gray sweatpants, they need to the thrown in the wash alongside the funky bedsheets, and my husband needs a good scrubbing.

"Is that for me?"

I almost jump out of my skin. "Shit, babe."

"Sorry. Didn't mean to scare you . . ." Ryan saunters into the bathroom as I stand from where I was kneeling tub side. He cradles a stem of luscious, round purple grapes from his dinner smorgasbord. With soft lips, he plucks one free, holding it between his teeth, and then leans over to kiss me, passing me the grape.

"You're good at that," I tease, the yummy juice bursting across my tongue. "I have a bag. For your arm. You stink."

He kisses me again, pulling me closer with his good arm. "I'm not getting into that tub without a chaperone. Doctor's orders."

"Whatever you say, Coach."

I help him out of the robe, out of his gray sweatpants and boxer briefs, and gingerly we tie the plastic bag around and under his arm, up over the shoulder. I use medical tape to adhere it to the skin along his upper shoulder, careful to avoid as many man hairs as I can. Maybe I should've shaved him first . . .

"Déjà vu," he mutters, watching me affix the plastic bag to his body.

I smile. He's referring to wrapping my arm cast, applied after a crow protecting its nest sent me sprawling and I inadvertently "rearranged" a couple of fingers on my left hand days before our wedding. Despite our efforts to keep my cast dry and clean, it was soaked with the byproducts of Elsbeth's unexpected entry into the world shortly after application. Yeah, that was a lot of gross. Let's not dwell.

"OK, you slide in first. Check to make sure it's not too hot." I help Ryan ease into the tub, keeping him upright so his bad arm's position remains stable.

He hums as he sinks into the water's warm embrace. "Damn, this is exactly what I needed."

"Not too hot?"

"Hot, but good hot."

I kneel next to him, checking to make sure the plastic bag is doing its job.

"Get naked," he rumbles. "I'm injured. I can't wash myself." He smirks like he knows the last number to a winning lottery ticket.

I make short work of my clothes—I contemplate another strip tease à la the failed Christmas attempt, but I'm not feeling particularly cute at the moment after a long day of work and catering to guests, plus the scandalous lacy number I alluded to earlier I'm saving for Valentine's Day. He will have to wait another six days for his own personal peep show.

No matter how blech I feel, Ryan always looks at me like I'm a goddess. At first I thought he was just being nice—his ex-fiancée could've been a bloody supermodel, for fuck's sake—but we've been together long enough now that I am confident the shimmer radiating from his eyes when he sees me unclothed (and clothed, for that matter) is beyond him wanting to be polite. He loves me. A lot.

And as I slide into the hot water, sucking air through my teeth to lessen the sting, he parts his thighs and bends his legs, steam rising from his exposed knees, so I can slide closer. Our face-to-face position looks like some mutant lotus—four knees jutting like islands from a tub-size ocean. I reach for the new bar of soap and lather up, starting with his shins to his feet, up the back of his calves to his thighs, down the incline to where his legs attach to his torso—

It's his turn to suck in a breath as my hand drifts over the forbidden fruit.

But then I move up his abdomen, still carved with athleticism, around his ribs, up his beautiful chest, under his good arm (I will let him wash under the damaged side), up and around his neck. He rests his head against the wall, eyes closed, that flirty grin twisting his lips that vibrate with the occasional moan of *Damn, that feels good.*

I remembered to grab a cup from the kitchen before disrobing. Slowly, gently, I scoop water to rinse away the soap, the tub clouding a bit, but not so much that I can't see the stimulating effects of my careful ministrations. Once Ryan is free of bubbles, I let the cup float, scooching myself ever closer, hands returning to my preferred target.

"How's your pain?" I ask, stroking with a light grip in case he's not into this.

"Getting better every second," he says, lifting his head from the wall, his eyes hooded. "What did I do right to deserve such excellent care?"

"You answered the phone when some crazy drunk girl from Portland needed a friend." I adjust my position so I'm sitting on my knees, not super comfortable thanks to the tub's textured anti-slip surface, and tighten my grip, speed up my cadence, watching Ryan's face for signs of anything but pleasure. Since water is not the best lube, I don't want to fumble a stroke and break his penis.

He lifts his good hand and cups my boob, tugging the nipple, kneading, uttering "I'm good, it's OK" upon the occasional wince from being jarred. "Damn, woman, I've missed you."

We've been together long enough that I know what he likes, and I have learned from the best how to be a full-service concierge.

Ryan's hand moves from my chest to my arm, and he pulls me in close for a hot kiss, though I don't interrupt my rhythm, balancing my weight on my knees, my left hand against the wall next to his head. His fingers find a hiding place of their own, and suddenly I'm in the game too.

He also possesses an encyclopedic knowledge of my erogenous anatomy, and right now—

*Bzzzzz. Bzzzzz. Bzzzzz.*

"I love you so much, Hols . . ."

*Bzzzz. Bzzzz. Bzzzz.*

My phone. On the quartz countertop in the kitchen.

I need to be louder so Ryan doesn't hear it and then maybe he will break through that finish-line tape and I can hop out and see who the hell won't stop calling when everyone *should* know that I'm off for the night, tending to my invalid spouse.

Any tingly shivers from Ryan's dexterous digits have fizzled to the beat of my buzzing phone. Alas, I moan louder so he will just—

He freezes for a three count, then disengages and cups my nape so he can kiss me hard. "Thank you . . . I love you, babe . . . Did you . . ."

I kiss him back. "I'm good. Let me help you rinse off. Do you want more hot water?"

The buzzing seizure restarts.

Ryan's eyes are closed as he pants, head back against the wall. "Is that one of our phones?"

"It's mine." Carefully, I ease back, stepping from the tub to wrap myself in a giant bath towel. "Don't move. I just need to see who it is."

"Can't someone else deal with . . ."

His voice fades as I hurry into the other room to see who the hell has *once again* interrupted us. If there ever comes a time when we decide to start a family, we will need to leave the country. Maybe the continent. ALWAYS interruptions.

"Hello?"

"Oh, hey, Hollie, it's Tabby. Sorry to bug you—"

"Is everything OK?"

"Well, Tanner was knackered, so he took Sarah and Els back to their cabin, and Miss Betty said she's feeling a little under the weather, and since Ryan is kind of out of commission—"

"Spit it out, Tabitha."

"Two guys just beat the shit out of each other in the lounge. One of them says he knows you. He's drunk and refusing to leave until he talks to you. Maybe if you come down, he'll finally go to his room."

"Does he not have a partner with him?" The weekend's guest register is all couples, given the themed package.

"A girlfriend, but she got pissed and won't answer their door."

"Who is this guy?" How would he know me? I don't remember seeing any familiar names on the reservations list.

"Can you just come downstairs? Oh, and we might also need some of your dad's Band-Aids."

# 8

The guy who "knows" me? His name is Joe Cirillo.
Mushroom Cap Joe.

He's a friend of Keith's, my long-ago ex, who is now happily married to a woman named Felicia (and father to a kid about the same age as Elsbeth), neither of whom I have heard from other than the occasional thumbs-up on superficial "look at my great life" Facebook posts. (Aren't most Facebook posts like that thin layer of pond ice? Not thick enough to walk on but if you look too deep, it's all murk and reality underneath.)

Mushroom Cap Joe, who allegedly earned his name because of his lack of endowment in the wiener department. I didn't give him that name—I never saw his wiener, thank the gods—but when I worked at 911 a million years ago, there were lots of jokes about EMT Joe and his teeny peeny, mostly because he fancied himself a ladies' man, was an absolute chauvinist among the ranks of first responders, and drove a growling, smoke-spewing truck with lots of Vs in its engine and tires taller than most Hondas. Oh, and he regularly referred to women as bitches and skanks, and not even in a playful, ironic way.

And while *yes*, it is not cool to make fun of people for their physical attributes, Joe has it coming. Super fun fella. A fungus on two legs.

Tonight, he's smashed out of his gourd, his likely broken nose bleeding on our lobby floor. And since his antics cheated me out of what could've been a satisfactory orgasm, I'm not super interested in his side of the story. The other dude, Lance something, wants to press charges, and while Bill, our facilities manager, and I agree that's not at all unreasonable, we don't have any RCMP on the island, and if we do summon a constable from the nearest detachment, both Joe and his sparring partner will probably end up arrested.

Tabby rejoins us in the lobby with a towel for Joe's nose and a crackable ice pack for Lance's swelling knuckles.

"I want a discount—no, a refund—on our room," Joe whines, shoving the corner of the towel up his nostril. "Keith said this place was above board, but you let assholes like this guy in—"

Said asshole moves like he's about to charge Joe again. Bill, Brad, and the two brawny maintenance/operations guys we call the Vikings (they're twin brothers who look like real-life Odins) form a human wall so no more fists can fly.

"Until we determine what happened and who started what, there will be no discounts or refunds or anything of the sort," I say, turning to Lance. "Please, if you're not in need of additional medical care, return to your suite and sleep this off."

Lance glares at Joe for another beat, shakes his head, and mutters "dick" under his breath.

Ha. If only he knew.

Brad and one of the Vikings (it's either Sven or Arne—I *still* cannot tell them apart) follow Lance out of the lobby, down the wide hall that leads to the guest quarters, and disappear around a corner.

"So, what, you're going to question your staff and then take that guy's side? I didn't throw the first punch. He was mouthing off about—"

My raised hand interrupts his sniveling. "Don't care, Joe. You've caused enough of a scene for tonight. If you are unwilling to go to your room, sleep it off, and start over tomorrow, I will have these handsome gentlemen escort you to the dock where you can wait in the cold for the RCMP boat to show up."

Joe snorts. "You don't have any Mounties on moose on your island?"

"Never heard that one before, Joe." I force a deep breath so other guests wandering past to head to their rooms don't see me losing my shit. "What's it gonna be?" Fake smile pasted on.

"You're still the same old bitch from before. Keith is so lucky he dodged that bullet."

I nod at Bill—*THE* nod—which means he will slip into the back office and radio the police, after all. The remaining Viking isn't touching Joe, but he's poised to grab him should he do anything stupid.

"And you're still the same old Mushroom Cap Joe everyone in dispatch made fun of for all those years. I'm surprised you're even here with a date. Does she know about . . ." I twirl my finger in front of his groin.

Thankfully, the Viking moves fast enough when Joe chooses to do something stupid.

He throws a drunken swing—and misses—but when the Viking tackles him, they knock me off my feet and I eat the front corner of the check-in desk.

Because of course I do.

# 9

"I didn't think he'd throw a punch." I suck in as my dad applies a Steri-Strip to the new cut along my cheekbone. When it heals, the scar will match the one under the other eye where the Christmas tree (or maybe the momma raccoon) left its mark back in December. The kitchen's first aid kit sits unzipped, its innards exposed to the world on the spotless silver prep table.

"You and your damn mouth," he mutters.

"What was I supposed to do? He called me a bitch."

"You were supposed to be quiet and ignore him because he's a drunken fool and you're a mature adult who knows better. It's a good thing Sven was there, or this could've been a lot worse." Nurse Bob, his hair askew since I obviously woke him from sleep, isn't gentle as he pushes an ice pack against my latest injury.

"Ow."

"You're a baby."

"Am not." My cheek throbs in time to my heartbeat. "How do you know it was Sven and not Arne?"

"You can't tell them apart?" Dad asks, shaking his head as if disappointed.

I stare at him for a second. "Why's your face so red and shiny?" He looks a bit like Santa in the off-season at the moment.

"Why are the RCMP here?" Ryan asks as he blows into the kitchen. He's managed to get a robe over his shoulders but his delicious chest is still bare underneath. "Hollie, what the—*why* didn't anyone call me?" He moves right up to me, a finger under my chin as he tilts my head to inspect my latest calamity. "What the fuck, Hollie . . ."

"I had it handled."

"Yeah, looks like it."

After we were so rudely interrupted during our bath time frolic, I helped Ryan out of the tub, into clean flannel pj pants, and then into bed where I dosed him with his evening medication allotment. I fibbed and said they were having issues with one of the credit/debit stations in the dining room lounge and that people were frustrated they couldn't pay and go to their rooms and that I'd be back in a jiffy, before his drugs sent him to Nigh'-Night Land.

What I didn't account for was the RCMP boat having its bloody blue spinning beacons cranked so that when they approached the island, the lights bounced off everything in the otherwise pitch-black night and flashed into the windows of our apartment that just happen to face east, looking over the water and docks and the whole shebang.

"What happened?"

"Mushroom Cap Joe."

"Who—do I want to know what that means?"

My dad hands me one of Elsbeth's yogurt popsicles, probably as a joke, but I take it and yank off the wrapper. Strawberry banana? *Fine.*

"This asshole from my former life is up this weekend. Old friend of Keith's. He picked a fight with some guy in the lounge and it got out of hand. Tabby called me, Bill and the Vikings were on it, but they needed Tanner or your mom or me to decide what to do."

"And you chose violence?"

"Yeah, I chose violence," I mock. Ryan steals my yogurt pop and takes a healthy bite.

"Where are the Vikings now?"

"With Bill, down at the dock talking to the cops."

"Do they know about this?" My husband points at my throbbing cheek and swelling eye with what's left of my frozen treat. Before I can answer him, the kitchen door opens and a Mountie in full winter gear strides through, notepad in hand.

"I guess they do now."

The constable—the patch on his left upper chest reads HARRIS—breaks into a smile when he spots Ryan. "Heyyyy, man, good to see you." He offers his hand for a shake and nods toward Ryan's bandaged arm. "Those hockey players just keep getting younger and meaner, don't they?"

The small talk lasts for a couple minutes so the constable and Ryan, clearly acquainted, can catch up. Then Constable Harris asks me questions about what happened, if we have security footage we'd be willing to download and share, the usual. I explain that Joe didn't physically connect with my face, that I fell as a result of the Viking stepping in, but Harris asks if I want to press charges anyway, and although Ryan answers yes when I say no, I reassure the friendly, chatty policeman that I'd just like Joe Cirillo to be removed and banned from our idyllic corner of the world.

"Freaking Americans coming up here all macho and shit," Harris says. "Good thing he didn't have his gun with him." He laughs at his unoriginal joke, clicks his pen, and after another round of handshakes, he's out the door.

Neither Ryan nor I comment on the fact that we're both American by birth, Canadian citizens by paperwork and the good grace of Her Late Majesty Queen Elizabeth (Canada is a British commonwealth). Also neither of us have guns. It is not a requirement of American citizenship to be armed, even if it appears that way to the rest of the world.

Whatever.

My cheek hurts.

And Ryan slobbered all over my yogurt pop. Very rude considering how I manhandled *his* yogurt pop not even an hour ago. Metaphorically speaking.

"Come on, Mohammed Ali. No more floating like a butterfly for you tonight." Ryan wraps his good arm around my shoulders, waves to my dad who's wiping crumbs off his shirt from another of Miss Betty's scones, and leads me back to our apartment. He's quiet the whole way, a smirk on his lips. I'm not sure if he's annoyed with yet another of my genius moves or if his painkillers have kicked in.

He opens our suite door and nods for me to enter first. "I have something for you," he says as I walk inside. "I was going to wait until Valentine's Day, but maybe you could use it now."

"If it's not an all-inclusive trip to somewhere with no other people and an endless dessert buffet, I'm not interested."

Ryan smiles. I wince with my return attempt since, as noted, my cheek hurts and my eye has swollen into a slit. "Sit."

I obey and sink into our very cozy couch.

"Close your eyes, or your eye, I guess. And no peeking."

Again, I do as I'm told. I hear a bit of one-handed maneuvering from across the room before Ryan sits beside me. I take a healthy sniff of his freshly bathed skin.

"Give me your hand."

"You're ready for that again?"

He snorts. "Smart-ass. I'm serious. Your hand, please."

I flatten my palm in the air between us and upon it he places what feels like an envelope.

"You can look now."

I do, and indeed it is a red envelope the size of a greeting card. Scrawled across the front in Ryan's signature chicken scratch: *OPEN ME FIRST.*

"What is it?"

He shrugs. "You gotta do what it says."

His face reveals nothing other than a satisfied smirk that a person gets when offering a present.

"Will I like it?" I tease my index finger under the seal, careful not to rip the paper (or my skin). Once open, I slide its contents free —a single flat card, nice quality card stock, like a Save the Date or RSVP card, its message printed in ornate script:

*Where Oliver frolics without a care,*
*And memories of Clara fill the air,*
*See where otters play and roam,*
*In your heart's collected home,*
*'Neath Enhydra's gaze, find me there.*

"Wait—is this a clue? Did you hide a present for me?" I push up from the couch with the card in hand, and the red envelope tumbles onto the area rug. "It is! This is a clue!"

I read it again, slower. "OK, I might be too dumb for this."

"Hardly." He snorts. "It took three of us to write that limerick."

"OK, Oliver . . . my tattoo! And Clara, our baby sea otter who's now a big girl . . . *'In your heart's collected home.'* Oh! My curio cabinet!" I drop the card onto the coffee table and bound across the room to the charming glass and wood collectibles hutch Ryan made for me after we got together. Inside on the four shelves sit my ever-expanding treasure trove of sea otters in all shapes and sizes.

I open the narrow doors and peer inside. The bottom shelf otters have been scooted to accommodate a perfectly square box wrapped in shiny red paper with a simple pink bow. "How did I not notice this before? When did you hide it?"

"I am very sneaky."

"Indeed, you are." I pluck the box from the shelf carefully. My prized pieces are made from glass, sandstone, compressed and carved volcanic ash, as well as wood, bronze, and even a gaudy rhinestone-encrusted, painted pewter otter that opens up to reveal a matching necklace in its belly. If there's a sea otter trinket in this world, my beloveds will find it and send it to me.

"Come. Sit. Open it before I fall asleep."

"Your drugs kicking in?"

Ryan bobs his head once as I ease back onto the cushion beside him. "Maybe I should share my pill sorter with you." He scrutinizes my latest fleshy insult.

"As tempting as that is . . . I'll be fine because you gave me a present!"

"So, are you gonna . . . open it?"

"But Valentine's Day isn't until next week—and I don't have anything for you."

Ryan leans over and lightly kisses me. "You're my Valentine, babe. Always and forever and every single day." Another quick kiss. "Now hurry up. I am seriously fading here."

The wrapping is lovely—I don't want to tear it—but his lids are about to slam closed on our evening. Paper removed, I gently tease the lid off the white cube. It's too big to be a ring box, plus Ryan knows I'm not a jewelry girl. He bought me a sparkly Canadian diamond tennis bracelet for our first anniversary and I promptly lost it. (It turned up again . . . a year later, in the couch, located when I was looking for Elsbeth's binky. Funny how you find stuff when you're looking for *other* stuff.)

A pillow of cotton fluff conceals whatever is nestled within. I pluck it free, and inside on a little blue pillow is another gem for my collection. "Ryan . . ."

I pull it out—an exquisitely carved and painted northern sea otter, her face and head blond, a perfect little black nose, with bristly, three-dimensional, wheat-colored whiskers dangling from her tiny cheeks. "Where on earth did you find her? She's my favorite!"

Ryan grins. "I had Matthias make it for you."

I look up at him. "Matthias the hockey player? From your team? Isn't he, like, seventeen?"

"He's eighteen, and yes, he carved it. His dad is a professional carver, like a real artist, so Matthias has been doing this stuff since he was old enough to hold a knife."

"She's . . . incredible." I examine every centimeter of the figurine. "I cannot believe a kid made this."

"Sweden has long winters. Said if he wasn't on the ice, he was carving."

I set the newest member of my *Enhydra lutris* collection on the coffee table and lean close to this living embodiment of perfection, speaking against his soft lips. "Thank you. I absolutely adore her. You are the best husband ever, Ryan Fielding."

He kisses me back, slow and languid. When he pulls free, his eyes beg for respite. "Happy early Valentine's Day, wife."

"I love you."

"I love you too. And I would love you even more if you would help me to bed because I cannot feel my tongue anymore."

I laugh and then stand to help him up from the couch. "When you're awake and relatively pain-free, you must allow me to show my gratitude properly."

He drapes his uninjured arm over my shoulders and we shuffle across the living room to our bedroom. "There is nothing more I look forward to than your demonstration of gratification." He practically slurs the words. I pull the sheet back, gently remove his robe, and ease him onto the bed. He settles into the mountain of pillows, a playful smile tugging at his mouth. "Speaking of gratification, there's more to Valentine's Day than one little otter."

I settle the sheet and the quilt over his legs and torso, careful not to put too much weight on his buggered arm.

"Oh yeah?"

"Just you wait, Porter. Cupid ain't got nothin' on me." His grin remains, even as his eyes close. With a soft hand, I push his wavy brown hair off his forehead and caress his bristly cheek with the back of my fingers. One more gentle kiss to his lips because I can't help myself, although bending over him reminds me of the pulse pounding in my cheek.

Mushroom Cap Joe would never do something so sweet as to commission a tiny hand-carved otter sculpture for the object of his affection.

Then again, I think tonight, the only thing Joe will be carving are his initials in an RCMP holding cell.

I love it when shit works out.

# 10

So rarely are we all together in one location—yes, Miss Betty and I live here full time and Tanner, Sarah, and Elsbeth are a boat ride away in their cabin—but Ryan is on the mainland months out of the year, and Dad lives in Portland and works way too many hours at the hospital. Point is, when it is declared that we will be dining as a family tonight, I'm thrilled.

Growing up, it was just me and Dad. And then me and Dad and Aurora the *very* strange stepmother and her daughter Moonstar and that *fucking goat,* omigod.

Yes. Mangala is still alive. He is, like, seventeen years old or something unnatural. I fear his evil will make him seventeen forever and he will never die and eventually he will become the head of the Volturi and rule over all the vampires with his lethal twisted horns and then when I am an old woman, Mangala will still be as evil as ever and, in fact, alongside his coven of ageless Italian vampires and a few sparkly cuties from Washington State, they will have taken over the government.

Wait. On second thought . . .

*Anyhoo,* tonight we're doing dinner, a proper dinner, in Miss Betty's apartment instead of the dining room where everyone has access to us to ask their burning questions about Ryan's injury, how his team is doing this year, or even *Hollie someone just hurled in the lobby restroom can you come handle it*. We have a houseful of romantic revelers with a two-for-one special on Cupid's Cure (it's red and bubbly and potent). There will definitely be some hurling going on, but Hollie Porter is *out of office*, bitches!

It's a tight fit with eight people (I invited Tabby because I do believe she is my cosmic twin from another dimension), and it smells *so* good in here. Miss Betty has a full-size kitchen in her place, so she's able to make two pans of her famous lasagna and fresh Italian bread to go along with it and a giant bowl of salad that looks tasty enough, *I* might even scoop some onto my plate, even if said salad consists of green things best served to rabbits. And immortal goats.

Tanner and Unca Ryan make a fort out of the couch cushions for Elsbeth and Acorn (rather, Unca supervises from a comfy armchair), though Acorn would much rather attack the cushions than hide under them, so the feat is rather Sisyphean. Tabby and Sarah and I sit at the dining table sipping a yummy Pinot and watch my dad and Miss Betty in the kitchen behaving as the grown-ups in the room—Dad does dishes while Miss Betty whips up whatever she's doing for dessert, the two of them talking about I don't even know what, but Dad makes Betty laugh so hard, she has to stop her whisking and bend in half for a beat.

Miss Betty has birthed four children. She says when she laughs too hard, she pees a little because "everything is loosey-goosey down there," which is way more information than I needed to know about my mother-in-law but also continues to freak me out about having children because I rather like everything high and tight in my undercarriage. Maybe I should mention to Dad not to make her laugh so hard or she will pee her pants for real.

Although watching them is nice. Dad is smiling, his heavy brow usually creased with the weight of the world smoother than usual, and Miss Betty—well, she always seems happy, though I know that's not true. She's been a widow and single mother since her Ryan and Tanner's father died over twenty years ago. That's why living at Revelation Cove has been so good for her. She has a whole new flock of ducklings to look after, and all this activity and frenetic energy (and all the people looking out for her) will keep her young and spry for decades to come.

Tabs has been filling Sarah in on the latest spa gossip, though I've heard it already in our running chat thread. My ears tune in when their convo transitions to talk of real estate. I raise my hand.

"I'm sorry, I was spacing out. Back up—are you guys moving?" I ask Sarah.

She looks over her shoulder toward her husband and daughter and indicates that I should keep my voice down. "Elsbeth needs to start kindergarten. She needs to be around other kids or else she will grow up to be that weird genius no one knows how to talk to."

"Those are the types who change the world," I say.

"Yeah, and they're weird as hell and completely self-absorbed and a little sociopathic. I don't want her to grow up isolated from the bigger world."

"I do . . . I don't want anyone near Elsbeth. She's too perfect."

"Ha!" Sarah laughs and sips. "She's five going on thirty. The kid needs way more than I can give her and there are only so many nature walks we can go on. She can name pretty much every plant and animal on our island."

"Your kid is way smarter than I will ever be," Tabby says, topping up her glass.

"So, are you going to Vancouver or . . .? Is Tanner leaving, because seriously, Sarah, this place will implode without him."

"No, no, he's not leaving. Nothing like that. And not Vancouver. We're only thinking about maybe Salt Spring. It's a tight-knit community and they have good schools."

"If you want her to be a certified genius, you should go to the mainland. Put her in one of those posh rich-people schools in North Vancouver."

I widen my eyes at Tabby in an effort to telepathically scold her for giving Sarah any ideas.

Our conversation is interrupted by Elsbeth's shriek and Acorn's bark—the pillow castle has collapsed and tickle torture is underway and I lock eyes with my boy toy sitting across the room and he gives me that smirk that warms up all my tingly bits.

"OK, good people of the village, it's time to eat!" my dad announces as Miss Betty pulls the second bubbling pasta pan from the oven and slides it onto a bamboo cutting board.

"I want more intel," I say quietly to Sarah just before her daughter bounds into her arms.

"It will all work out, just as it always does." Sarah, the eternal optimist. Elsbeth crawls across her mom and into my lap, singing her latest musical composition that I think was probably borrowed from Our Lady Taylor Swift but includes original lyrics about Acorn and sea otters.

That's my girl.

&.

The table is elbow to elbow, except Ryan who gets lots of space to avoid jarring his boo-boo. The confabulation barely slows, only to allow diners to take a bite, chew, moan about how good it is, and then inhale another forkful. Dad teases Miss Betty about how she should start a franchise with this lasagna recipe; Miss Betty counters about not wanting the headache of having to figure out what to do with the billion dollars that would flow in.

When we reach the part when we're mopping our plates with what's left of the bread so as not to waste a single drop of sauce or cheese, Dad taps the side of his wineglass with his spoon. The table silences, although Elsbeth is intrigued by Grampa Bob's attention-grabbing maneuver and lunges for the nearest utensil, only to give a searing glare at her dad when he moves her water glass out of her reach.

"So, this is a good time for my big announcement, since we're all together."

I stare at my father—a big announcement? He has said nothing prior to this moment about this, and we text back and forth daily. He smiles at me, revealing the bit of green stuck between two front teeth. I'm about to gesture when Miss Betty hands him a water glass and says, "Swish."

Nurse Bob obliges without skipping a beat. He smiles again for the whole table. "Better?"

We nod our approval.

"OK, so, as I was saying before I was so rudely interrupted by a rogue piece of basil, um, I am . . . retiring!"

The table erupts with cheers and congratulations. Elsbeth finally reaches a glass and bangs her spoon against it, the tinkling bordering on aggressive. She's gonna break—

Sarah smoothly relocates it.

"Retiring?" I ask. "Are you sick? Oh my god, are you having health issues and you just didn't know how to tell me?" My throat tightens. Ryan grips my shoulder and squeezes gently.

"No, no, honey, nothing like that. I'm just tired of the bureaucracy, the long hours, the canceled time off, and the young hires—I don't want to sound like a stereotype, but our new staff are a bunch of babies. They complain about everything."

"Oh, I hear that loud and clear," Miss Betty replies.

"Dad—" I intervene before the two of them spiral into a conversation about boomers and Gen X versus millennials and Gen Z because I require further elucidation on this truth bomb he's just dropped.

"So, wow, you're retiring. That's good," I say, my words probably meant to calm myself more than him. "You'll have more time for yourself, then, to do stuff you've always wanted to do but were too busy being Superdad."

"Hear! Hear!" Sarah says, lifting her wineglass. More tapping and tinkling of glassware. (This must be very confusing for Elsbeth.)

Dad sips and scans the attendees, pausing on the youngest member of our party. "I'm not retiring so I can sit in a La-Z-Boy and watch bowling. I'm actually starting a new business. My own business. Figured it's time to step into the twenty-first century and become a *solopreneur.*"

More cheers and applause.

Except I'm worried—if he knows that word, he's probably been spending too much time on social media, maybe taking advice from slick-haired scammers who promise a million-dollar business is possible in just five days if you open an Etsy store or hawk some manner of essential oil or green health powder. The snake oil salesmen of yesteryear would be so envious of their modern-day brethren.

"I am still going to be working in healthcare. My new business will involve an outreach program where I will visit nursing homes, assisted living facilities, anywhere a senior member of our population would live after moving out of their primary residence. I'll be providing education and resources about sexual health for those of us later in life. From there, I will arrange sessions at community centers for seniors who do still live independently in the—"

"Wait." I interrupt. "What does that mean?"

"That means your dad is going to teach sex ed to horny old people," Tabby interprets. "I think that's an *awesome* idea, Nurse Bob. Just because you're wrinkly and slow doesn't mean you don't appreciate a visit to Jiffy Lube now and again."

Tabby's response is met with giggles, but before I can clarify, before I can wrap my head around the visual of my father standing in front of a group of septuagenarians, sliding a condom over a banana or narrating a slideshow about genital warts, Miss Betty chimes in.

Of course she does.

"I, for one, think this is a brilliant idea, Bob." She pats his hand where it rests on the table and then looks back at all of us. "Not all my 'kneads' can be met by baking alone." Except when she says *needs*, she mimes kneading bread, and the table groans and quickly moves into awkward chuckles. I am unsettled as images of sweet Miss Betty taking it from behind flashes on the screen in my brain.

"Who wants whisky?" I jar the table in my haste to stand.

"I do!" Elsbeth shouts.

# 11

"But why didn't he tell me ahead of time?"

"Probably because he was worried what you would think." Ryan leans back into pillow mountain. Due to his current condition, alcohol is a hard pass. I cannot say the same for myself, though I did stop after two—three?—to ensure his safe return to our marital bed.

With Ryan sorted, I move to my side and begin my own preslumber ritual. "He's my dad—he knows I would do anything for him, that I support whatever decisions he makes."

"That might be true, but you seemed a little freaked out after his big announcement."

"Forgive me for having a moment where I couldn't stop envisioning my dad talking about orgasms and syphilis in front of a group of old farts."

"If you're lucky, you will be an old fart one day."

"You know what I mean." I toss my bra across the padded bench at the end of our bed.

"Are you telling me that when we're dropping our teeth in a glass before bed that you're not going to let me touch those fun bags?"

I laugh. "Babe, when we're old, you aren't gonna wanna touch these fun bags. They'll be more like sad thrift-store Samsonites by then."

Ryan's turn to chuckle. "Hollie Porter, I will always want to touch your Samsonites. Even when I'm a toothless geezer."

"Well, you are considerably older than I am, so when you're ready for elder care, I will be, what, thirty-seven?" Carefully, I slide under the bedcovers and nudge as close to Ryan as I can without bumping his arm cradled across his chest. "Also, I plan on keeping my teeth."

"Is this where I insert a joke about dentures and blow jobs?"

"Oh my god, *stop*. Please. And do not make that joke to my dad —he probably has some statistic about dentures and blow jobs, which is why he's becoming a sex fairy to randy pensioners." I lean up on my elbow to look at his face. "How's your pain?"

"I'm good. Mild headache. Arm's fine. Blowing out my knee was way worse. This is just annoying." He nods at me. "How's the eye?"

I shrug. "It's a black eye. I'm more worried about the cut leaving yet another scar."

"Scars are hot. They make you look tough."

"Yeah, great, because tough is the look I was going for."

Ryan snickers and then nudges me to move down, pulling at the pillow under my head.

"What, you want service? Now?"

"No, perv. Scoot down a bit so I can play with your hair."

"Oh. Well. OK, then." I accommodate, positioning myself so he can run his fingers through hair that probably could use a wash. My husband knows how to relax me, his fingertips light against my forehead and temples.

"This is a good thing, Hols. Your dad looks happy. Relieved to be leaving a job that has been wearing him down for years. And if he thinks he can build a business around teaching safe sex to old folks, more power to him. I'd be interested in sitting in on one of his—"

"Nope. Nope. Nuh-uh. If you need instructions on how to use a penis pump, I have an iPad in the kitchen and a VPN. I will find you whatever you want."

Ryan flattens his warm hand against my cheek, the bed shaking with his laugh. "You're all the penis pump I need, Hollie Porter."

More romantic words have never been spoken.

"Babe . . ."

"Mmm."

"Hollie." Soft fingertips tug on my earlobe. "Your alarm is going off."

My eyes resist opening but my eardrums engage and sure enough, my wake-up call chimes from my nightstand. I awaken in the same spot I dozed off, my limbs heavy from lack of movement.

"You snored last night."

"Did not." I push up and grab my phone to silence it before flopping back on my pillow.

"That's a good thing. Means you slept hard. Or it means you're developing sleep apnea, which isn't so good."

"Why are you awake?" I ask, cracking my eyelids to look over at him. "Wait—you're up already? Are you hurting? Is everything OK?"

"Everything is fine. I woke up at four and couldn't get back to sleep, so I've been watching game tape and answering emails."

"Answering emails."

"One-handed typing sucks."

"You could've just waited for me. If you dictate, I can type."

"Not necessary. Besides, you were out. You would've slept through an earthquake."

"Don't joke about earthquakes. You know how I feel about the island cracking in two and sliding into the ocean, taking us along with it."

Ryan smirks. "I made coffee. Get up."

I slide deeper under the blankets. "I don't wannnnnna."

Ryan's weight lifts off the mattress. "Then I guess I will just have to find someone else to give this next present to."

I throw the blankets back. "You got me another present?"

"Every day until Valentine's Day, my queen."

"Shut up. You did not."

He winks and walks away, pausing at the door threshold to wiggle his luscious ass in those sinfully tight gray sweatpants.

"Tease." But it works. I jump up, quickly shower and brush my teeth, and throw on my robe. It's just after six a.m. I've still got time to dress and paint my face to be at the front desk by seven when the breakfast buffet opens.

Ryan stands at the kitchen island, coffee cup in hand, eyes glued to his laptop.

"Is that yesterday's game?" I ask. They lost in overtime. Nils texted as we were finishing dessert. Tabby tried to act cool, but I always notice the sparkle in her eye whenever Nils's name comes up.

"Yeah." Ryan pauses the video and nods at the steaming cup he's poured for me, its contents the perfect shade of light brown. Gotta love a man who knows exactly how you like your morning caffeine injection. "Your next clue." From his back pocket, he pulls a red envelope, a twin to the one from last night, and slides it across the island.

It reads *OPEN ME SECOND*. I do, of course slicing open my flesh on the paper because why not. I suck on the line of blood so I don't smear it on the card as I release it from its crimson sheath. Again, the clue has been printed in ornate calligraphy on heavy card stock. I'm impressed. This took some serious planning.

> *Where the Salish whispers tales under the moon's soft glow,*
> *In a vessel of escape from a storm long ago,*
> *Spy-hopping orca need not appear,*
> *Pressed sand creates a receptacle so clear,*
> *To hold the murmurs of love's words so dear.*

I read it a second time, aloud. "OK, so—this has something to do with the water, maybe the rowboat I stole that night?" Ryan grins and sips his coffee, watching me puzzle it out. I reread the last two lines again in a whisper.

"This is, like, a legit treasure hunt," I say, grinning.

"It is."

"I need to get dressed and go look!"

"That sounds like a fun idea."

I pop off my stool and *carefully* lean on tiptoes to kiss my beloved. "Come on, then. Let's get moving."

Ryan's goofy grin doesn't disappear as I help him dress—except when I stop to examine and apply soothing lotion to the fresh chafing around his neck from his arm sling. I tell him to ask my dad about it when they have their next PT session, which right now only involves *very* gentle range of motion so his shoulder doesn't seize up. Until the headaches subside and his arm bone has had a chance to graft, Ryan's on limited duty—and he's gonna get bitchy about what he's not allowed to do here soon.

I'm applying a final coat of mascara to my twelve eyelashes when my phone lights up on the bathroom vanity. A text from Dad:

> Maybe overindulged on too much good food and drink. Feeling a little shaky this morning. See you at lunch.

My dad rarely drinks, and I only saw him sip a single pour of the pricey Dalmore.

> Is it food poisoning? Can I bring you anything?

> Nothing like that. Don't fret.

Except I will fret a little because at Dad's last thorough physical, apparently his cholesterol is elevated (he blames too many staff birthday cakes), his blood pressure has been on the high side (he blames stress from staff who are always taking days off to celebrate said birthdays), and his sugars have been flirting with diabetes (refer to aforementioned cakes).

Ryan pauses in the bathroom doorway. "Ma'am, will you kindly lace up my boots?" Our eyes meet in the mirror. "Why are you biting your lip? What's wrong?"

"Nothing, it's fine." I drop my mascara into my makeup bag. "My dad says he's not feeling great." I show Ryan the text.

"He did eat two servings of the lasagna."

"Yeah, no, I know . . . I just worry. Now that he's announced his retirement to the universe, I'm worried a heart attack will try to take him out like a rogue wave. You hear about that happening all the time—"

Ryan steps behind me and wraps his arm around my chest, both of us facing the mirror. Every time I see us together in a reflection or photograph, I want to pinch myself. How did I get so lucky?

"Stop worrying. Nurse Bob is healthy as a horse and too stubborn to do anything but exactly what he wants to do—and that does not include heart attacks."

We stare at each other for a few beats until I'm distracted by the toothpaste spatter on the glass.

"If it would ease your worry, let's go down and make him a plate, grab some Tums or aspirin or whatever, then you can take it to his room before we resume your treasure hunt."

"You wouldn't mind?"

"Absolutely not." He kisses the top of my head. "Now please double-knot my shoes so I don't trip and break something else."

# 12

I don't know what medications my dad has been prescribed, but given his occupation, I'm sure he has a handle on whatever he's supposed to be taking. Although he is a guy—and men are notoriously stubborn about self-care until body parts gravely dysfunction or fall off.

I can't tell you how many times he's tried to go into work only to be diagnosed with pneumonia when he arrived for his shift, breathless and wheezing from the walk across the parking garage. All it would've taken is a single glance at his reflection to notice he looked on the brink of death. It's a good thing he's surrounded by so many professional women who don't put up with his nonsense. They've probably saved his life on more than one occasion.

I have a tray loaded with fresh tomato juice, a bottle of sugar-free Gatorade, peppermint-ginger tea, buttered white toast, a banana, two scrambled eggs, even a steaming bowl of chicken broth, just in case. Chef Joseph knows how to put together a rescue breakfast. In a small plastic cup, I have two each of Tums, Tylenol, and Advil. Bases = covered.

The second treasure hunt clue is burning a hole in my pocket, but Ryan and I agreed to meet up in half an hour to proceed with my adventure. Tray balanced on my arm—a skill that has only taken me the past five years to master—I greet resort guests in the wide halls on my way to Dad's room.

I stop at his door and raise my left hand to knock but then pause. What if he's asleep? I don't want to wake him. The meal is covered with a silver warming bonnet so everything will be edible for another hour at least. I could just leave it on the small dining table and he can eat when he wakes up. I put my ear against the door to listen for a TV or even him on his phone.

It's quiet.

From my keychain, I fumble with the master key card and gently ease open the door. The rooms are designed like most hotels—the bathroom on the right or left upon entry, the main sleeping chamber just after. We always try to give Dad one of the multiroom suites, but he insists on a regular guest room so we can save the suites for paying guests. Straight ahead upon entering, a rustic wood, two-person round table sits in the corner. I'll just leave the tray for him—

Except as the bed comes into view, I am witness to a scene no child should ever see their parent in.

Even worse, the scene involves my husband's parent too.

"Oh! Oh my god, I am so sorry—" I back up too abruptly and smack my elbow into the forty-five-degree angle where the walls join and Dad's breakfast topples with all the grace of a china cabinet in an aftershock, egg and juice and broth and tea flying everywhere and not at all in slow motion.

I drop to the floor, my head down, hurrying to gather the spilled tray contents, mumbling "Oh my god, oh my god, I am so sorry," over and over again while Miss Betty fumbles for the blanket to cover herself. My dad bounds off the bed and throws on what I hope are boxers but Jesus, I'm not about to look up. Seeing his white ass in the air like that—

*No, no, no, no, no, LA LA LA LA LA.*

"Hollie, leave the food. Just go on and we'll clean it up."

"Right. Sorry, Dad. So sorry, Miss Betty. I'm leaving now." On all fours, I pivot and crawl, head down, toward the door, fumbling with the handle to get it open so I can escape. Once I'm in the hall, breathless, my face on fire, I lean against the wall, hand over my galloping heart.

On the other side of the door, my father and Miss Betty burst into laughter.

"You're making a bigger deal out of this than it is," Ryan says, placing a glass of OJ in front of me.

"I am *not*. If you'd walked in on that—seeing our *parents* doing—"

"Stop. One replay is more than enough for this lifetime." Ryan rounds the island and sits on the neighboring stool. "I mean, yeah, it's embarrassing to walk in on anyone doing that, especially your dad—"

"And your *mom*."

Ryan brings his coffee cup to his lips.

"Wait—if they're a couple, does that mean you'll be my stepbrother? I think there are laws against that. We're *married*, Ryan. We cannot become stepsiblings."

"It was sex, Hollie, not a marriage proposal."

I stand from my stool, arms crossed over my chest. "You are not upset enough about this."

"What is there to be upset about? Is it a little weird that our parents are hooking up? Yeah. But isn't it also kind of cool that your dad, who is younger than my mother, is offering her something she has been without for years?"

My rebuttal withers on my tongue. Miss Betty has been a widow for a long time, and though she's told me on a number of occasions that she was so in love with Ryan's dad, that they were soul mates, she's confided that she was resentful after he died, that he didn't take better care of himself and stop the smoking and drinking so they could grow old together.

"Now you make me sound like a swamp-dwelling goblin who hates love."

Ryan laughs and gestures for me to drop my pout and step closer. I do, resting my cheek on his broad shoulder. "I cannot scrub the image from my brain. My dad's ass cheeks are *really* white."

"I doubt they see much sun. Maybe we should tell him about Wreck Beach."

"Oh sure, that's a great idea. Then he and your mom could go sunbathe nude *together*. 'Bob, can you help me with sunscreen right here—'"

"Got it. Thank you." He kisses the crown of my head. "I am sorry for the trauma you experienced this morning, my darling wife." He nudges me back and touches his nose tip to mine. "At least our parents have excellent taste. I mean, I can hardly keep my hands off you."

I kiss my mister, the taste of coffee on his lips. His signature scent, woodsy and clean with the spicy fragrance of a new beard oil he's been trying, revs my engine. "OK, yes, I will concede that point. I can see why they'd be attracted to each other."

Ryan feathers his lips over mine. "And no one is getting married."

Another kiss. "So we won't be stepsiblings."

He licks my upper lip. "I'd still want you, even if you were my stepsister."

"Ew," I say. "We are neither vampires nor the royal family."

He smirks. "Are you prepared to get back to this morning's first order of business?"

The treasure hunt! I'd forgotten about it in my desperation to bleach my brain after the breakfast delivery gone awry.

I pluck the card from my back pocket, glad it was not dislodged in my haste to escape, and read it once again.

"Follow me, sir."

# 13

The morning breeze is brisk, as one would expect just six weeks into a new year, but the air smells so fresh, I will never take it for granted. I grew up in Portland, so I'm more than familiar with big-city scents, but on our island, it's all trees and sea and birds all the time.

I am endlessly grateful to be allowed to live at Revelation Cove, and in Canada, for that matter, even if sometimes it is lonely with Ryan in Langley for the Giants' hockey season *and* if I still can't help giggling whenever a Canadian pronounces *Mazda* or *drama* or *llama* with that funny *a* (*draaa-muh* vs. American *draw-muh*). However, right now, my Prince Charming is home, and with my arm looped through his, we're moseying down the walkway toward the docks under a mostly cloudy but not menacing sky as if we have all the time in the world, and there isn't a Mazda with llama drama anywhere in sight.

When we passed through the lobby and bid good morning to our staff already situated at their battle stations, only two guests paused us to ask Ryan how he's feeling, about this year's playoff run for his team. And being the consummate professional both on and off the ice, Ryan responded with the charismatic charm that turns first-time guests into regulars.

Miss Betty wasn't at the front desk like she usually is this time of the morning, but we are not thinking about where Miss Betty is or what she's doing because she's a grown-ass woman, as am I, so if my mother-in-law wants to have a leisurely morning in the arms of her lover, so be it.

*Shudder.*

"Stop thinking about it," Ryan teases.

"I'm trying."

Ryan pauses where the concrete yields to the engineered-wood planking of the docks. "Lead the way, Mrs. Fielding."

"See, that doesn't help. Mrs. Fielding is your mother. And your mother is currently getting drilled into a mattress by my—"

"Hols, stop. Seriously." He shakes his head. "Shared trauma is great and all, but now you're being mean."

"Sorry. I'm just wondering if my dad will want to legally adopt you so that we're full siblings—oww!" I slap at his good hand pinching my muffin-shaped pooch currently defying the boundaries set by the waistband of my uniform cargo pants. What can I say—a good man, good food and drink, and unfettered access to the resort's pâtissier have filled out my pear shape nicely.

"Please lead on, my precious princess." As if to punctuate his request, his stomach growls loudly. He will require sustenance imminently.

With the clue card cupped in my palm, I read it through again and set off down the dock toward where the rowboats should be tied off. Except, duh—our dinghy fleet has been pulled from the strait for winter, stacked three high on the double-sided steel frame under a metal-roofed canopy.

"My rowboat has been decommissioned," I say.

Ryan simply bobs his head once.

"You're not going to give me anything else?"

He mimes zipping of his lips.

That night when I commandeered the small wooden boat, I'd been completely unprepared for the strength of the current and had no idea an impressive thunderstorm was en route. I was feeling sorry for myself thanks to a sprained ankle from ill-advised shoes, my newly single heart stinging from betrayal of that slimy businessman who showered me with attention and innuendo, at least until he showed up in the dining room with his perfect wife and children and I morphed into an invisible idiot with one pathetic smirk delivered from across the dining room as he pulled out her chair.

In hindsight? Thank the gods it all went down that way. Pretty sure Roger Dodger's moved on to another trophy wife and left the first one (and their two kids) fighting for alimony. I hope she sues for punitive damages too—Roger was way too tan for a man his age, in this climate.

But to the task at hand—if my dinghy is out of service, the next logical place to look would be the cabin cruiser Ryan rescued me in that fateful night. He remains quiet, his lips playfully twisted as I slowly step backward in the direction of the boat. *Yes*, I'm mindful of where the dock ends and the water begins so I will not be providing further entertainment in the way of a slapstick tumble into the strait. I've done that plenty of times already so it's not really funny anymore.

I pause alongside the Fielding family vessel and point. "Am I getting warmer?"

"Sweltering."

Carefully, I step onto the outboard deck and unzip the canvas cover protecting the stern seating area. Before stepping inside, I turn to Ryan. "You want help boarding?"

"I'll wait here. Go find your treasure."

Every time I set foot on this boat, I think of that night when Ryan rescued me, the nights we've spent in the forward cabin in various stages of undress, the many times we've gone to observe my beloved sea otters, even our wedding day when Ryan secretly arranged to have the ceremony on Otter Beach instead of at the resort . . .

I still get choked up thinking about that day, how incredibly kind and thoughtful he was, how, from the first moment I met him, Ryan

Fielding has always looked out for me. Especially when Lucy Collins, my long-lost mother, reappeared and tried her best to upstage every single thing. Looking around the interior of this boat that's been in the Fielding clan for years, it's nothing but good memories. The best.

"You OK in there?"

"Yup!" I should probably look around.

Cupboards, crannies, under couches, in the cozy privy, and lastly in the forward cabin.

I should've checked their first.

It's where we first revealed our compatible body parts to each other. That was a fun night.

Smack-dab in the middle of the bed sits a brown paper gift bag, its exterior decorated with what look to be hand-drawn hearts and flowers. I collect the red-ribbon handles and exit the cabin, not peeking into the bag until I rejoin my husband. "Found it!"

"About time. I was about to drop a crab pot to see about getting myself some breakfast."

"Har har." I rezip the canopy and step onto the dock. "Should I open it now?"

"I thought that's what you were doing inside."

"No, I wanted to give you the joy of watching me discover your creative generosity."

"I would love nothing more."

I stick my tongue out at him and kneel on the dock. From within the craft-paper bag, I extract a big jar, clear glass, a big red bow wrapped around its lid and mouth, the inside filled with tiny paper cranes in every color of the rainbow. I recall part of his clue: *Pressed sand creates a receptacle so clear.* "'Pressed sand'—you meant glass!"

"Indeed."

"Ryan, you are so damn smart."

"I did all right in eighth grade science." He nods at the jar as I stand. "So, this present has a rule."

"A rule?"

"Kind of." He taps its side. "There are three hundred and sixty-five birds in here. I tried to do origami otters, but they were too complicated." He twists off the lid and pulls out a single pink crane and hands it to me. "Unfold it."

"But . . . it's so cute. I don't wanna ruin it."

"It's OK. Go ahead."

I set the jar back into the paper bag to prevent any chance of catastrophe and then carefully unfold the origami. "I can't believe you folded all these . . . how long did it take?"

"It's not polite to ask how the sausage is made."

"Mmm, sausage." I waggle my brows suggestively and eye his crotch.

With the last fold undone, I stare at the perfect square of paper, upon which is a message:

***Because you make me laugh every single day.***

My eyes and nose sting. Ryan closes the distance between us and wraps his hand around my nape. "Three hundred and sixty-five reasons why I love you. So, the rule is, you can open all of them at once, or you can dole them out, one a day, like a Valentine's advent calendar."

"Ryan . . . are you serious?"

"Do you like it? Is it super dorky?"

"Dude, come on. This is genius. You're the best fucking husband in the entire world." I tuck the note into my vest pocket and gently hug my man as the happy tears carve tracks in the freshly applied foundation that's already doing a woeful job of concealing my black eye.

Worth it.

I tip my head and meet his lips. Even his peepers are a bit glazed with emotion.

"How is this real life?" I whisper.

"Happy early Valentine's Day, Porter."

As we reenter the lobby, a blast of heat skitters over our chilled cheeks and fills our noses with the sumptuous aroma of morning food. The space is busy—guests heading into the spa or down the hall to the heated outdoor pool and hot tub or lined up at the concierge desk to sign out a pair of binoculars to do some wildlife watching from various spots on our island. We don't offer day cruises until April, though our winter guests are sometimes treated to a passing pod of transient orca. We have plenty of birds of prey in the neighborhood, as well as great blue heron, owls, and deer. Lots of creatures for our photography enthusiasts to fill their memory cards.

We haven't had a cougar sighting up here since Chloe, but that doesn't mean the feisty felines aren't hiding in the forests of nearby islands. (Fun fact: Vancouver Island, south of us, has the highest concentration of cougars anywhere in the world. And those suckers can swim.)

My sea otters (they're not really mine although yes they are) north of here, we leave alone most of the time. As a critically endangered species, they don't need human looky-loos disrupting their days. I will occasionally sneak up the strait to check in and count them, but that's with the express permission of Fisheries Canada. I learned my lesson after rescuing baby Clara.

The stream of humanity parts, and Miss Betty comes into view behind the front desk, smiling as she chats up a guest.

"Act normal," Ryan whispers in my ear.

Easy for him to say.

As we approach, Miss Betty's eyes light up at seeing her baby boy. "Good morning!" she chirps. "How're you feeling?"

Ryan releases my hand and steps behind the counter to hug his mom and kiss her cheek. "I'm good. We're just about to have breakfast. Have you eaten yet?"

I choke on my spit and launch into a coughing fit.

She would've eaten breakfast had I not spilled it all over the carpet of my dad's room.

"Um—" Cough, sputter. "I'm gonna—" Suck in a squeaky

breath. "Put this away first—" Still coughing, I hoist the gift bag. "Meet you in the dining room."

I leave before either has a chance to protest, coughing into my sleeve so I don't freak out anyone standing too close. Only I would choke on my own saliva with enough spirit to make it sound as if I'm dying of TB.

Just as I'm passing the sitting area, I notice Acorn in front of the fireplace, his paws wrapped around whatever toy he's chewing apart. I've never seen a dog go through toys the way he does.

Except—this toy—it's bright pink and it seems he's tearing off small chunks, pausing to chew like it's bubble gum before tearing into it again, the floor around his big paws littered with mutilated pink nuggets.

I approach, whispering so I don't restart the coughing fit. "Hey, buddy, what you got there? Did Miss Betty order you more goodies?"

I set my gift bag down slowly—if Acorn suspects he's in trouble, he'll bolt and take his prize with him. That's fine if it's a chewie toy he's supposed to have but not so fine when it's the remote control to the nearest TV. We've gone through at least a dozen in the last two years.

Except our remotes aren't typically neon pink.

"Whatcha doin' there, Acorn—"

Ohhhh, shit.

It's not a chewie toy or a remote control.

He's currently disassembling a vibrator that I'm almost positive belongs to me.

# 14

A corn misunderstands when I try to take his "toy"—his doggie brain thinks I'm inviting him to a rousing game of tug-of-war, even though I'm really just trying to get this thing away from him before anyone notices or before he somehow activates it and it drops to skitter across the floor.

"Hollie Cat!" Elsbeth shouts from across the lobby. "Goo' morning! I'm here!"

*Yes, of course you are.*

She runs toward us and I strong-arm the vibrator from Acorn's mouth and drop it into the paper bag with my jar of love-soaked paper cranes.

"What are you guys doing?" Elsbeth rests a hand on my shoulder as I feverishly gather the torn pink chunks from the area rug. "Acorn, did you eat another toy?"

"Yup, he did."

"I'll help."

"NO!" In unison, Acorn barks and Elsbeth startles, her eyes widening. I have to divert before we move to full-on lip-wobbling, followed by the first tear. "I mean, Auntie's gonna clean it up. Have you had breakfast yet?"

Elsbeth sniffs and wipes at her eye. I scared her.

But I'm picking up pieces of silicone likely coated with unnamed germs from unmentionable body parts and now dog slobber on top of that—

"I'm sorry, baby girl. I didn't mean to yell. I just don't want you to get your hands icky, especially before breakfast."

"That's OK, Auntie. Mommy told me on the boat that you're having a tough day so that I should give you a hug as soon as I found you. And I found you!" She throws her arms around my neck and nearly topples me. I hug back, though careful not to touch her adorable North Face coat with my hands.

And if Sarah has told her child that Auntie Hollie is having a tough day, that means Ryan texted his brother to share this morning's salacious breaking news.

"Never a dull moment with you around, Hollie," Tanner says as he walks up behind us.

"That's why you pay me the big bucks." I'm still kneeling, balanced on one bent leg, trying like hell to cover the silicone chunks with the heel of my boot, even as Acorn nips and paws at my hand.

Elsbeth lets go of me and leaps into Tanner's arms. "Food, please, Daddy."

He raises an eyebrow at me and smiles at his daughter. "Yes, ma'am." Tanner then notices that I'm grabbing at chunks of unknown origin. Acorn thinks we're playing. "Did he chew up something he wasn't supposed to?"

"Yes." That's all I'm gonna say. "I got it. You guys go grab some food before it's all gone."

"Come eat pamcakes with me, Hollie Cat!" Elsbeth's tiny voice bounces off the ceiling.

"You save me a seat and I will be right there, OK? I'm just gonna clean up this mess."

Finally, they walk away, Elsbeth telling her dad how I scared her with my big voice but that I didn't mean it and it's just because Acorn is being a bad boy again.

I roll this golden repeat offender onto his back, checking

underneath him—sure enough, he's hiding bigger pieces of pink silicone. "You really are the worst dog, you know that?"

He stands and barks right in my face, dropping into a front bow like he's about to pounce, his tail whipping so hard, I fear with a few steps to the left, he will knock over the small vase of flowers on the coffee table behind him. Since I don't have any dog treats in my pocket, I quickly scan the area for any other distraction—aha! An actual Bully Stick he's *supposed* to be tearing apart.

I lunge and grab it, giving it a light toss across the sitting area, hoping he will give chase.

He does not. Only barks again, spraying me with dog breath.

"You cannot eat any more of this silicone," I growl at him, dropping every little piece into the bag to keep it out of his reach. I have no idea if silicone is dangerous for dogs—I mean, it has to be, right? Even if the stuff used on sex toys is considered food grade?

I need to go back to the apartment and see how much pink skin is missing from the device, i.e., how much is in this dog's stomach and what the ratio is of dog to silicone before it necessitates a trip to the emergency vet.

I'll need to tell someone. Miss Betty mostly cares for Acorn, so I should mention it—except then I have to explain what the dog ate, and I've already had one awkward encounter with my mother-in-law this morning.

Ugh.

Acorn finally loses interest when he realizes I'm not in the mood to roughhouse. Once I'm confident every pink shred has been plucked from the rug and surrounding area, I stand, my knees popping as I straighten and reach for my wonderful gift bag that is now filled with the remnants of—

"Hols."

I spin. "Dad."

He smiles. "Good morning."

"Hi. Hello. Good morning."

"Don't make this weird," he says, straightening his shirt.

"I'm not. It's not—it's fine. Everything's fine."

"We are consenting adults."

"Oh my god, Dad, you just said not to make it weird." I move to push past him but he gently grabs my arm.

"Betty is a wonderful woman. You know that."

"Yes, of course. That's great. I'm glad you're happy, that you're both happy."

Dad smiles again, and although he's trying to stay frosty, I can see the hint of embarrassment in his eyes.

"I just didn't need to see that part of your person"—I gulp and look at the ceiling for a beat—"first thing in the morning. Or ever, on any morning."

"It was very sweet of you to bring me breakfast."

"I thought you were sick. I was worried."

"Fit as a fiddle," Dad says, lifting his arms to showcase his hale and hearty self. He then notices the bag in my hand. "What's that?"

"Oh, it's just a Valentine's thing from Ryan."

"He's a good man. Apple doesn't fall far from the tree."

"Got it. OK, thanks." I can't make eye contact or keep the grin off my face as I step away. "Wait—" I pause. "Since I don't know that I could be any more traumatized than I already am this morning, how much do you know about dogs and silicone?"

❦

My dad takes the lead on explaining to Miss Betty what Acorn did —she blushes almost as hard as I did after stumbling into their love den—and then he examines Acorn the best he can, considering he's a nurse for people and not canines. He suggests we call Acorn's vet, which Miss Betty does, delicately explaining that the dog ingested food-grade silicone without explaining in full where said silicone originated (or what it's likely seen in its lifetime).

The three of us are in the back office as she "Mm-hmms" and "Yes, sure, that makes sense" into her phone. Behind her, our wall of video monitors show a resort full of happy people. I understand that I am an adult, that my father and Miss Betty are both adults, but I don't know if this situation could get any more bizarre.

"OK, thank you so much, Dr. Welton. Say hello to Chris for us."

She slides her finger across her phone screen. "So, she said we are to watch his poops, see if the silicone passes. If he vomits or stops eating, then we need to take him in for scans. He could develop an intestinal blockage, depending how much he ate before you found him."

"Wonderful." A spike of pain pings up the side of my head—I'm clenching my teeth again.

"Do you not have the offending item in your bag there, Hols?" Dad points at the gift bag hanging from my fingertips. "We could try to put it back together—"

"Great idea. I will do that. You guys just watch his crap, yeah?"

Dad snorts and shakes his head; Miss Betty hides her smile behind her hand.

"Right then, good seeing you both. Busy day ahead. Make sure to eat!" With that, I'm out of the back office, practically sprinting down the hall so no one else attempts to stop me for idle chitchat about my dad's sex life.

Once in our apartment, I hoist my precious jar of origami birds from the bag, pluck an antibacterial wipe from the tub on the counter, and give the exterior glass surface a thorough wipe-down. I want to be able to touch it without being grossed out that it was in the bag with my dead vibrator.

From under the sink, I pull out a pair of nitrile cleaning gloves. Another double layer of paper towel spread on the kitchen island will serve as my operating table as I attempt to reconstruct the sex toy to estimate how much silicone is gurgling in Acorn's gut right now.

Dumb dog.

A sea otter would never eat a vibrator.

Acorn successfully degloved the main shaft and little rabbit head so that the mechanism itself is almost completely exposed. And there is no way I'll put this puzzle back together, not when many of the pieces are no bigger than my thumbnail. I stare at it for a few minutes, google the brand to see if that might help visualize, and then realize I could waste all day unraveling the mystery of the murdered vibrator.

I have a million other things to do. Cupid's Cove Ball is scheduled to start in mere hours.

I roll the deceased device into its paper towel shroud and deposit securely in our garbage can. I know we have a bin for recyclable electronics, but I don't know if this qualifies and I'm sure as shit not going to ask Bill, our facilities manager, or any of his crew. The Vikings would never let me live it down. I'm still finding paper cutouts of angry raccoons hidden here and there—and the Vikings weren't even present at Christmas to watch Momma Raccoon's assault happen in real time.

Hands washed, I make a quick cup of coffee and (try to) fix my face so I can get to work. The jar of winged love notes winks at me from the kitchen island—it's very tempting to pop the lid free and unfurl all the other reasons my incredibly thoughtful husband loves me—but patience is a virtue. Good things come to those who wait. Rome wasn't built in a day.

OK, no idea what Rome has to do with anything.

Before rejoining the troops, I pause to tidy the bedding and rearrange pillow mountain. The sun brightens the room but also highlights dust on everything. Maybe I should see if Elsie wants to earn an extra hundred bucks and clean for me this week. I open the drawer to the nightstand to put away my eyedrops and ChapStick—

And freeze.

My vibrator, the hot pink one with the long bit and the titillating bunny ears is sitting in its spot, intact, unmolested, unchewed by dog teeth.

Which means the one Acorn eviscerated belongs to someone else.

# 15

A corn pooped.
A lot.

I still don't know whose vibrator he ate. I'm afraid to ask.

And I scrubbed a layer of skin off my hands once I realized it was not, in fact, my intimate instrument of ecstasy.

Last Saturday's Cupid's Cove Ball was a hit—just as we expected, lots of drunk people, loads of fun, great music provided by our staff band, the Garden Gnomes, who have been practicing every available moment since our Christmas fete (and it shows). Also, the addition of the Vikings, one twin on keyboards, the other on lead vocals, has helped tremendously.

Our first weekend of Valentine's revelers have returned to their lives and the next wave, many of whom are here for the "Galentine's Day" package, is arriving as we speak. Tabby is freaking out about accommodating all the mani-pedis, facials, makeovers, and massages; I told her worst-case scenario, we'll send the Vikings in to help.

The Galentines would *love* that.

Tomorrow is February 14, and *I'm* trying not to panic because Ryan, as he promised, has presented me with clues that have led to unbelievably cool gifts every day since the first one last week. I now have a gift certificate for a tattoo session with this insanely talented artist in Victoria who is impossible to get time with (its envelope was taped to the underside of the table in the main dining room where Ryan soothed my ego after Roger humiliated me); an excursion package from another Discovery Islands company that includes a sea otter viewing trip and photography lesson over an eight-hour day (hidden in a fake book on a bookshelf in the sitting area near the lobby fireplace); a huge "Gardener's Delight" gift box of seeds so I can start my own respectable vegetable and flower garden this year in a square of the land that used to be golf course (cleverly stashed in the—what else—garden shed); and last night—OMG— the hint took us down to our seasonal fake-ice rink, to center ice, where, sitting on a box of brand-new, fancy white figure skates was the puck from Ryan's first-ever NHL goal.

Isn't that the *sweetest* thing you've ever heard?

It made us both cry. The puck, not the skates. Although the skates are cool too. (It's more of an inside joke about how I suck at skating and always use the excuse that I'm wearing borrowed hockey skates so now, evidently, I don't have anything standing in my way of Olympic stardom.)

And then, after I thanked my husband *thoroughly* for his unrivaled kindness, I placed the puck—its edge wrapped in athletic tape with the game and date written in Sharpie—in the otters-only curio cabinet because it is very special and I cannot believe he gave it to me.

I mist up just thinking about it.

Hence why I am currently fluttering about like a one-winged moth because I have done nothing nearly as awesome for Valentine's Day for my hunky heartthrob. Sure, the lingerie I ordered is spicy, but how lame am I that I ordered a strip of lace and silk when he has given me *so* much?

I have totally blown it this year.

And now the lobby is filling with fit women in red-soled, four-inch heels who spend more on their nightly moisturizer than I do on my annual clothing budget. We get a lot of attractive, monied people staying here, and usually I can quiet the bitchy voice in my brain who whispers how I should try harder if I want to keep my man, but today, the head harpy is yelling like she's a *Titanic* survivor trying to summon a lifeboat.

It doesn't help that the fleshy insult from Mushroom Cap Joe's tantrum last week got a tiny bit infected, likely from me using my unwashed makeup brush to try to cover it, and so my dad has had to squeeze antibiotic goo into the pink-edged wound and now I look practically pubescent and my period is imminent so I have other spots to make my face resemble a dot-to-dot.

And yet, Ryan Fielding continues to profess his undying love.

If his farts weren't so rank and he didn't snore so loudly from that misaligned nose, I'd say he's too good to be true.

Alas, one of these days, I will defeat this insecurity monster who shares my skin.

But in the words of Aragorn in Peter Jackson's highly celebrated film, *Return of the King,* just before the good guys engage in the Battle of the Black Gate, "[I]t is not this day!"

Perfect, considering the guest who just walked in, surrounded by her posse. Nicolette Meyer. Gorgeous, blond, rich, mean like a feral barn cat.

We hosted her wedding a few years back, but a day or two before the ceremony, she "accidentally" speared her fiancé in the calf with an arrow during an archery outing, and then at the part of the nuptials when the pastor asks for objections—usually a rhetorical question—one of the groomsmen declared his loudly, so a huge fight broke out. Ryan used the airhorn we keep on hand for wildlife deterrence, the bride and groom did not get married, and we had enough leftovers from disappointed guests who skipped the non-reception to treat the whole Revelation Cove team to a decadent meal.

That was actually kinda fun.

What was *not* fun was how she treated my staff.

Even now, several years post incident when one would hope maturity might have calmed the poor dear, Nicolette Meyer aggressively taps a manicured fingertip on the polished surface of the front counter. I am standing at my laptop beside young Hannah, who slides into action.

"Welcome to Revelation Cove! Can I get your names?" Hannah didn't work here when Nicolette Meyer made her first impression on our team, but that doesn't stop Ms. Meyer from sighing and rolling her eyes, as if we should *all* know who she is.

I step in. "How are you, Nicolette? Good to see you again."

"We have a two o'clock with your spa," she says, gesturing to her four friends. "We need to get to our suites and settle in so we're not rushed."

A quick glance at the clock on the computer screen shows it's only 12:18, so plenty of time to "settle in," though I don't dare say anything. Whenever I experience the urge to snark back at someone, I hear Miss Betty in my head: *They are paying guests, even if sometimes you'd pay them to leave.*

Hannah and I make quick business of handing out key cards and Valentine's gift bags. I summon Cam, our very handsome concierge, to assist Nicolette and her party since everyone else who doubles as a bellhop is otherwise occupied. Nicolette's face lights up when she sees Cam approach—he has that effect on sentient humans of all ages. I must remember to warn him about her retractable fangs.

As if she's read my mind, Hannah leans close and whispers, "She looks like Rosalie Cullen."

I laugh, earning myself an over-the-shoulder glare from Nicolette that would scare Nosferatu.

ॐ

By dinner, I consider googling the penalty for murder in British Columbia.

Three goals by a single player in a hockey game equal a hat trick, and obviously, that means the player is having a good game. However, I know the saying goes that bad luck *also* comes in threes. And I've had my three for this week: walking in on my dad and Miss Betty, the dog eating the vibrator and pooping all over the place,

69

and Nicolette Meyer stepping back into her role as pampered, spoiled diva, as if those shoes were awaiting her return by our front door.

Granted, if she did have shoes waiting by our front door, Acorn would've decorated them with danger biscuits.

Whatever. I've dealt with my share of prickly guests during my time here at the Cove. But Nicolette makes problematic into an art form. In the salon, she didn't like her mani-pedi and said our tech was too rough on her cuticles and the shade of pink wasn't the one she chose, so the poor girl had to redo all twenty nails with nary a gratuity in sight. (In fact, Nicolette insisted we comp the service, refusing to pay for "shoddy work.") Then in the spa, the sauna allegedly smelled "weird," the towels weren't soft enough, she was mad Tabby ran out of lavender mask and refused to use anything with cucumber or mint and then lectured the spa staff about how superior the Korean skincare products are and that we should really be sourcing from overseas instead of local Canadian products that just aren't as good. In the dining room, she harassed the waitstaff about not enough Aperol in her spritz, about how the butter in her scallops tasted like margarine, how we really should have a gluten-free option for the baguettes (we do and even offered her one), and she made sure everyone around her knew she's American and her dad is a *very* important man in Portland and Los Angeles and how they really should've gone to Palm Springs instead of coming all the way up here to freeze to death with a bunch of lumberjacks.

*Thou shalt not harm your guests.*
*Thou shalt not harm your guests.*
*Thou shalt not harm your guests.*

If I close my eyes and tap my heels together three times, will Nicolette Meyer disappear?

The Garden Gnomes are halfway through a closed rehearsal in the ballroom for tomorrow night's Valentine's Day dance, though given the proximity to the lobby and front desk area, their jam session is still loud—just muffled. I offered to hold down the fort so Hannah could practice with the band (turns out she's handy with a tambourine), which means I am hanging out in the back office scheduling social media for next week on my laptop while watching *Schitt's Creek* on my iPad, in between helping guests who ding the desk bell with their random requests.

Speaking of *shits*, Acorn is mostly back to normal, other than fouling up the joint from the antibiotics and stool softeners the vet gave him. He's eating and drinking and running around like a raver on Molly, plus his poops are no longer pink-sprinkled. He will live to see another day.

Miss Betty and my dad are entertaining some Cove regulars in the lounge, and every now and again, I hear Dad's laugh above the din. I'm glad he's having a good time, and I've never seen Miss Betty's eyes sparkle so much. It's fine. It's just a Valentine's fling. I mean, Dad can't actually *move* here, can he? Because I don't think Miss Betty has any plans to head south. She loves living on the island.

Right?

Ryan keeps telling me not to worry about it so much, that it's healthy and good for our parents to have "alone time," even if it is still weird that *his* mother and *my* father are having "alone time" and we don't even live in Alabama so I'm not sure what the protocol is. Rather than fretting over it as much as I am, my insouciant husband is in our apartment live-streaming his team's game, coaching via FaceTime, despite the doctor's orders that he's not supposed to be watching screens or elevating his blood pressure.

As sweet as he's been this last week, and as much as I've *adored* having him home, he's counting down the seconds until he gets back to his team. And we've had a few more conversations about what it would look like if I were to leave Revelation Cove and join him in Langley, at least for the rest of the hockey season. I'm not totally ready to return to civilization full time, and Ryan has no interest in selling his stake in the resort, so we're trying to have our cake and eat it too.

"Excuse me, hello . . ."

Ugh. I know that voice. I pause my show right as Alexis Rose is about to launch into her spirited vocal audition for *Cabaret*.

"Hello!"

"I'm right here. Sorry, just doing a little work. How can I help you, Nicolette?"

She flattens her palms on the front desk counter and leans into it. I don't need to see her eyes to know she's hammered—her breath confirms it. "Why isn't the ballroom open? We can hear the music. My friends and I want to dance."

"They're rehearsing for tomorrow night, for the Valentine's Day party."

"Fine, but tonight is for *Gal*entines, and my *gals* and I want to go in and let loose."

"That's why tonight we arranged for the romantic comedy movie marathon in our smaller ballroom. We have a popcorn machine and open bar and tons of bean bags and comfy pillows to cozy up with."

"We're not fourteen"—she squints at my name tag pinned above my left boob—"Hollie."

Wow. I'm not even important enough for her to remember my name, despite the *many* phone and email hours I spent helping her plan her (failed) wedding?

"The lounge is open until one a.m., the outdoor pool is heated, and as you know, your suites have hot tubs. If you're interested in our special Galentine's Day dessert, I can grab a menu—"

"I've had enough sugar and carbs to last a lifetime." She drops a hand over her perfectly flat stomach. "I am so bloated from the food your chef made. Is he even a real chef?"

My fingernails carve crescents in my palms. "Nicolette, is there anything I can do for you tonight? You sound like maybe you're having a rough time."

She glares at me, and I give her the smile I would give a bear before it charged. And then, out of nowhere, Nicolette Meyer starts sobbing.

# 16

She cries so loud and so hard, I don't know what to do other than pull her into the back office so she doesn't attract a crowd.

"Where did your friends go? Can I call or text someone for you?"

She slumps into one of Miss Betty's floral wingback chairs. "No, don't call any of them. They're not even my real friends. They're just people who hang out with me because I'm rich."

I pull one of the wheeled office chairs from the desk under the wall of monitors. "Would you like some coffee or tea?" I gesture to our small caffeine station.

"Do you have any vodka?"

"Not back here, sorry." I grab a box of tissues and hand it over. She stares at it for a beat, as if trying to figure out what it is, and then takes it.

"Do you have any idea how hard it is to be me?"

"Um, no, I don't. I'm sorry you're struggling. Are you sure you don't want to talk to a friend about this?"

"No! I don't have any friends. Jesus, don't you listen?" She slurs and attempts to straighten in the chair as she wipes at a dainty blob of clear snot running from one nostril. Even her nasal mucus is pretty. "Those women are only here because I'm paying for everything. They're the girlfriends and mistresses of Daddy's friends. He thought it would be good for me to get away with some *gals* instead of sitting in my penthouse, feeling sorry for myself that my fiancé is fucking his secretary."

Yikes.

Hold up—which fiancé are talking about?

Nicolette Meyer carries on through the remainder of the Garden Gnomes set list. Apparently, after her matrimonial mayhem a few years ago, she and Edwin (the groomsman who declared his objection) immediately shacked up together and got engaged, the whole nine yards. They've been planning a destination wedding (another one? You'd think her parents would spring for a taxi to the courthouse at this point) in the Maldives, but then a couple weeks ago, Nicolette arrived home early from a Paris shopping trip and found Edwin and his barely legal secretary tangled in Nicolette's Egyptian-cotton penthouse sheets.

"Am I cursed when it comes to men? Like, what the hell is wrong with them? I'm hot, I've got my own money, I don't mind anal—like, I'm the full package. I just don't get it."

"Yeah, wow, I don't know. That sounds like you're dealing with a lot." Every ninety or so seconds, I glance at the security camera feed, hoping I will spot Nicolette's posse stumbling out of the lounge to come collect their sloppy leader.

"Sometimes I wish I could just be a normal person. Someone like you. A boring job, you don't have to worry about fashion because you're always wearing this uniform, you don't care about the gray hairs growing in or that your eyebrows look like sickly caterpillars."

Wait—what? Gray hair? And what's wrong with my eyebrows?

"You can eat whatever you want and you don't care what it does to your skin or your ass because you're not going to charity galas and red-carpet events all the time, so it doesn't matter if you have to ask your stylist to have the designer send over the size 4 instead of the 2."

"Mm-hmm, I hate it when that happens." She's insulted me

enough now that my flirtation with compassion has devolved into a date with sarcasm.

Nicolette plucks another tissue from the box and blows her nose.

I am so pleased to hear it honk like a Canada goose.

"I just want to be in love, ya know? My parents have a terrible marriage. They both cheat all the time and they both know it, and then Daddy will bring home the chlam and Mother gets angry and calls her private doctor for another round of doxy and then they fight about who gave it to who. Constant fighting."

Oh god, her tears are restarting.

"Do you know who my favorite person in our house staff is? The gardener. Luis. I mean, we have a lot of gardeners, but he's in charge. He's my favorite because he's always smiling, even though his job is dirty and sweaty and he works all the time, no matter the season, because he has a big family and lots of kids and they're all grown up now, so he has grandkids. He had a hip and knee replacement last year and still came back to work for us, not because he loves gardening but because he needed the insurance coverage for his wife. She's got breast cancer." Nicolette sobs harder. "It's the only time I've ever seen Luis not smile—when he told me about his dying wife."

This conversation has taken an unexpected turn.

"Like, I look at those people and they have so little. They live in an old subdivision with a bunch of crappy old cookie-cutter houses and the only reason Luis drives a nice truck is because Mother was embarrassed about him driving his piece of shit to our house every day, so she leased him a pickup."

"Luis sounds like a good man."

She nods. "I want that. I want a good man. I want someone to take care of, someone who will take care of me too. I don't want to fight every single day over stupid shit. I don't want my man to screw other women. I don't think human beings are supposed to go through life alone. Do you?"

"I think a person has to spend a little time finding out who they really are in order to find success in a relationship."

"What, like, go to therapy? I have a therapist. He always stares at my boobs."

"Well, *that's* inappropriate. Maybe it's time to find a new therapist."

"Maybe." She *hmmphs* back in the chair, grabs a perfect curled end of her hair, and feathers it over her lips. For a moment, she looks like a little girl. "I might be single forever."

"I doubt that very much. If you're open to finding a relationship, it will happen, but it has to be with the right guy—not just some hottie who's after your money. Do some work on yourself, figure out what you like, what makes you happy. Don't settle for abs and a pretty face. You never know—the love of your life could be about to bump into you around the next corner."

She honks into a Kleenex wad again. I pull the round garbage can from under the desk for her to throw away her snot rags. "Are you still married to that hockey player?"

Ha, so she *does* know who I am. "Yes, I am still married to Ryan Fielding."

"Is he a good man? Like, are you guys in love?"

I grin. "He is a very good man. And we are ridiculously in love."

"You're lucky. I don't think I've ever been in love for real. After Rob and I broke up and Edwin moved in, I needed some space, you know? So I took a month and tried my own version of that movie with Julia Roberts—*Eat, Pray, Love* or whatever. Totally overrated. I ate so much in Italy, I had to custom order a new wardrobe while I was there. The praying part was dumb—totally humid and there were bugs and we weren't allowed to talk. And the love, oh my god, what a joke." She hiccups on a sob.

The front desk bell rings.

"I'm so sorry—one sec, Nicolette. I just need to see who that is."

She snorts and nods. Maybe I should get her some Gatorade. And Advil.

I round the corner to the desk and find my dad standing at the counter. "Sorry for the bell. I texted you." He smiles that dad smile that makes me feel warm and safe.

"Yeah—no, I'm just . . ." I throw a thumb over my shoulder toward the back office. "Did you have a nice evening?"

"We did. So much fun. I forget how great it is to hang out with normal people." He chuckles. "Is Ryan in your apartment? I was going to check on him, make sure he's keeping up with his medications."

"Dad, you are not on duty tonight. You're supposed to relax."

"I know, but I would sleep better if I checked real quick." His phone buzzes from what sounds like the pocket of his blazer. I told him he didn't need a jacket for dinner, but knowing what I know now, I think he's dressing to impress.

Sure enough, he plucks the phone free, reads the screen, and his dopey smile widens.

I will guess it's from Lady Marmalade—

*Ding! Ding! Ding!*

Marmalade? Like, jam? Miss Betty makes the world's *best* jam? How did I not put two and two together?

"I'm off, then. See you at breakfast . . . in the dining room?" He winks and hurries down the hall.

"Hollie? You should come here," Nicolette calls.

What now? Oh god, she's gonna barf.

I step across the threshold into the quaint back office to find Nicolette standing in front of the wall of security screens. "What is that?"

She points at one of the monitors.

It's the camera down at the seasonal fake-ice rink.

Shit, shit, *shit* . . .

"That, my dear Nicolette, is a cougar."

# 17

I'd call it an unfortunate coincidence that we have a mountain lion on the island after what happened with Chloe, but this *is* British Columbia, and as I mentioned before, we have a significant concentration of the tawny, long-tailed pussycats in this part of the world. And given my and Ryan's prior bitey interlude with *Puma concolor vancouverensis* at Tanner and Sarah's cabin, we definitely have wildlife procedures for Revelation Cove.

First thing, I alert Bill and his crew, which initiates the lockdown of all exterior doors and requires anyone in the pool or hot tub to come inside. I then quickly record a warning message in our phone system; that message is subsequently sent to the landlines in every room and suite, followed by a text message to all our guests' cell phones and a banner warning across the guests' messaging system. This all happens in under five minutes.

All while I try to calm the PTSD pirouetting through my nervous system as I caress the scarring on my left forearm from Chloe's handiwork.

Both the private staff and open guest chats catch fire. Everyone wants to see the cougar, which is fine, as long as they do it from within the safety of our four walls.

Nicolette Meyer sits transfixed in the back office, watching the screens and sipping the Gatorade I fetched for her from the kitchen. "Will it come up here to the lodge?"

"I don't know. It's probably just looking for a place to snooze before resuming the hunt."

"Didn't you get bitten by a cougar or something? Was that you or am I thinking of someone else . . ."

"Yeah, it was me." I don't want to go into details. I, too, am watching the camera feed from the rink where the cat is now sprawled on the fake ice, leisurely bathing itself. If I didn't know firsthand how lethal these animals are, I'd think it hilarious that it grooms itself like a house cat.

"Hey, babe. You good?" Ryan breezes into the back office, pausing for a sec when he notices Nicolette in front of the surveillance wall.

"There's a cougar!" she announces.

"You notified Bill and all?"

"Of course."

He kisses the side of my head. "Well, as long as everyone stays inside, we'll be fine. The cat will get bored soon enough when it realizes we don't have anything delicious to eat."

One of the Vikings—still no idea if it's Sven or Arne—walks in.

"I'd say there's plenty delicious to eat," Nicolette purrs, her attention transferred from the cougar to the Norse warrior in our midst. "My god, you are a huge man."

Sven/Arne hikes his bushy brow at her and then looks back to me. "Patio and deck are cleared. Only a few people were in the hot tub and they're inside now. What else do you need me to do?"

Before I can answer: "You know what, Hollie, I am feeling a little woozy from all those cocktails, and now that you have a *cougar* on the premises, I'm scared for my safety," Nicolette says, leaning against the desk dramatically. "Do you think this—"

"Arne," the Viking answers.

"Do you think this *Arne* could escort me to my room, just in case that big kitty has found a way into the lodge? I'd hate for anything to happen that could lead to a lawsuit."

I look at the Viking—Arne. He shrugs.

"Come on, then," he says.

"Ohhhh, and he's bossy." Nicolette collects her long blond hair over one shoulder as she crosses the space that feels very small all of a sudden. Arne steps over the threshold, and Nicolette pauses before me, seemingly freed from her existential crisis. "Thanks for the girl talk. Also, whatever foundation you're using, it's the wrong shade. Your cheek looks green on one side."

She sashays out, hips engaged, as if the last hour of her sobbing through an entire box of tissue didn't happen.

"What was that . . ." Ryan looks through the doorway and then back at me.

"I'll tell you later." From the desk drawer, I grab my powder compact and pop it open to examine my skin. She's not wrong. My cheek and under-eye are still healing.

I wonder if that cougar would be interested in a little Nicolette au Vin. Maybe Nicolette à l'Orange. Soufflé au Nicolette?

Nah, that's mean. I'd never do that to the poor cat.

# 18

Our newest resident—Congratulations! It's a boy!—spent the evening scent-marking the property. The closest he got to the building was the walkway outside the front doors. We've been watching the camera feeds closely all night, and though we've not seen him in the last two hours, we're not a hundred percent sure he's moved on.

So, this Valentine's Day morning, instead of lying naked and satiated alongside my groom, I am in the back office on the phone with the Conservation Officer Service. It's an absolute last resort in my books—if they can't encourage the cat to leave, they may have to shoot it.

Wildlife murder is not great for business.

Except Conservation can't arrive until this afternoon, and there's no way our guests will be happy about being stuck inside the lodge on a day that has dawned as stunning as this one.

My dad raps on the open door and enters the back office while I'm still on the phone. Nurse Bob has brought me a breakfast tray this time, although he manages to keep it upright as he slides it onto the desk.

Finally, I hang up and practically dive into the steaming coffee. "You're the best."

"Any updates?"

"Our facilities manager is waiting for Tanner to arrive and then they will do a circle of the island in one of the boats, then on foot if they don't spot him."

"That seems dangerous if the cat is still here."

"They have rifles. And cougars are usually afraid of people."

"Let's hope you're right. I'm supposed to be on vacation."

From the tray he plucks a second mug, the tea string for Earl Grey draped over the rim. "How's Ryan this morning?"

"He seems good. No pain, at least not that he's telling me about. When I came down here, he was on the phone with Nils already, so yeah."

"No taking the hockey out of that boy." Dad smiles and gestures to one of the wingback chairs. I nod; he sits. "You've been avoiding me. I want to talk about—"

"Dad, it's fine. Whatever. We don't need to talk about anything." I pop my head out of the office to make sure Hannah is at the desk to help our guests and then click the door closed. I don't want anyone overhearing this conversation.

"I know it's been a bit odd for you to see Miss Betty and me flirting and hanging out this last week."

I close my eyes for the count of three, instantly regretting it as the image of my dad's white ass flashes against my eyelids. "Dad, seriously—"

"Hollie Cat, sit down for a second."

*Please don't tell me you're getting married.*

"We're not getting married," he says. Uncanny how he does that. "But it's more than just a Valentine's fling. We are dating. Long distance. Betty has been an amazing friend over the last few years. It's like she breathed new life into my world. I'd gotten a little stuck, I think, after Aurora took forever with the divorce and everything at work with budgetary restrictions and staffing issues—I think I was in burnout and didn't even realize it because I'd been running on autopilot for so long."

I finally do take a seat. This sounds more serious than I thought.

"Betty and I started texting last year after I came up for Canada Day weekend, and it's grown from there. She's an incredible woman. She cares so deeply for everyone in her life, and she makes me laugh every time we talk."

My throat tightens as I think of the first folded crane I opened from the love jar. Ryan wrote the same thing about me on that square of origami paper.

"Anyway, she's the one who encouraged me to think outside the box, to question why I'm giving so much of myself to the hospital. Yes, I love my coworkers—most of them—and helping people brings me so much joy, but the administration side of things . . . Hospitals are a for-profit business. They don't care that they're cycling through staff and burning people out. All they care about is making money."

A telltale red brightens my dad's cheeks—he's about to wind himself up. And as much as I don't want to dive into the best-kept-private details of my father's love life, I also don't want him to launch into a diatribe about the injustices of the American medical system.

"Dad, again, I am so sorry I walked in on you guys. I know I'm an adult and I should be able to just brush it off, and I will—it was just a little . . . unsettling." Nicolette Meyer's words from last night echo in my head: *I don't think human beings are supposed to go through life alone.* "So, if being with Miss Betty makes you happy, then you should go for it. Life is short and all that jazz, right?"

He snickers. "You have no idea how short it is, kid." He sets his tea aside and stands, pulling me from my chair for a hug. "I love you, Hollie Cat. You are the best human I know."

I laugh into his shoulder. "You're just saying that so I'll comp your breakfast."

"Nah, Betty already took care of that." His laugh bounces off the walls of this tiny office as he pushes back to chuck my chin with the side of his finger. "I promise we will try to make this as not weird as possible."

"Ryan and I want you guys to be happy. But it will get totally weird if you decide to tie the knot because then Ryan and I will be stepsiblings. That seems illegal to me."

"Well, at least you know Betty can't get pregnant."

"Aaaaaand you went there," I say, backing up and opening the door. "Have a pleasant day, Mr. Porter. Please remain indoors until we are certain the cougar has been relocated otherwise."

My dad collects his mug from the side table and pauses before me just as he's exiting.

"It's all right. I have a cougar of my own."

# 19

Apparently, it's good to know people in positions of influence. Constable Harris, the responding officer when Mushroom Cap Joe misbehaved, really likes Ryan. So Ryan called to ask if Harris had any pull with Conservation to get someone to come to the island sooner than this afternoon since our furry feline friend seemed uninterested in paddling across the Salish Sea to partake of the well-stocked black-tail deer buffet on nearby shores.

Lo and behold, Harris's brother-in-law, Joey Dunmore, is the head Conservation officer assigned to our neck of the woods.

So Harris called Joey and the cavalry arrived, and instead of lead, they shot our cougar with a tranquilizer, obtained blood samples and affixed a tracking collar, and then whisked him off our island via boat for relocation farther north. Many of the guests whined about why they couldn't go out and watch; Constable Harris made a general announcement in the lobby about the legal repercussions of interfering with law enforcement and Conservation officers in the performance of their duties.

Being the smart-ass I am, I unnecessarily added that I'd be happy to show pictures of Ryan's destroyed arm after our prior run in with Chloe. That shut people up. (Except for this one lady who actually did want to see photos and I told her I was only kidding and that maybe she'd enjoy a complimentary mimosa instead.)

With the Adventures of Cagey Cougar concluded, the Valentine's dance is once again front and center. As part of the staff, I'm expected to greet everyone as they join the party, and though my face will ache at evening's end from the permasmile and polite head-bobbing, it is fun to see everyone in their Valentine's finery, a fashion palette that includes everything from sequined, ball-worthy gowns to leather pants, from playful sparkly tights to fuzzy red and pink sweaters paired with iridescent angel wings.

I'm in a hot red satin number, tighter than is safe for work, but it's not meant to stay on my person all night. Not if I have my way.

The ballroom sparkles as if Chef Joseph has used a cannon to blast the whole place with lusty—ahem, *luster*—dust. In addition to her duties as the spa and salon manager, Tabby took on the role of chairperson for the special events planning committee, and not a moment too soon. I was running out of clever ways to use streamers and that annoying glitter confetti you can buy in bulk from Amazon.

Ryan stands with his good arm draped casually over my shoulders as we make the rounds. Tabby bounds onstage and welcomes everyone, telling a few jokes to warm up the crowd, promising a good time with the open bar serving Cupid's Cure all night and urging partygoers to eat as much as possible so that she's not left with the temptation of leftover pastries once everyone goes home.

And then, as if they choreographed the timing of their entrance —which they must have done since the lights dim and a spotlight shines at the doors and *oh my god*, the Garden Gnomes launch into a version of "Lady Marmalade"—my dad and Miss Betty saunter in. In front of a captive, whooping, applauding audience, they stroll to the center of the dance floor and take their bows. It's like this is prom, the votes have been counted, and they are crowned queen and king.

Dad is dressed in a three-piece suit, the shimmery, off-white fabric printed with red and pink hearts of varying sizes and shapes. And Miss Betty looks glorious in a fifties-style swing dress with an off-the-shoulder, cinched-waist bodice and a crinoline underneath to volumize the skirt.

They *match*.

I clap until my palms sting and holler until my throat aches. Ryan laughs so hard, he's crying, although I do wonder if the moisture seeping from the corner of his eye is inspired by how gorgeous—and *happy*—his mom looks.

The Garden Gnomes wrap "Marmalade" and slide into the next song of the evening, a slow oldie that must mean something to Miss Betty and Nurse Bob, since they've only got eyes for each other.

All right, yeah, it's still a little weird, but *oh my god*, they look so cute.

With each successive number, the crowd forms a pretty even split between romantic and raucous. The couples here to celebrate their undying love sway in tight hugs on the dance floor, no matter the tempo of the song, while the Galentines keep the bartenders busy and the beats pounding. They get especially excited when the Gnomes drop into a Shania Twain cover, the volume deafening as Gals of all ages yell along with the chorus about how they feel like a woman.

And Nicolette Meyer? She eyes Viking Arne, the microphone clutched in his hand as he croons through the set list, like she's going to devour him before night's end.

Ryan and I don't risk the commotion of the dance floor. He takes my hand and leads me to a darkened corner where no one can bump into him with a misdirected Cupid Shuffle. With his good arm wrapped around my waist, he presses his forehead to mine.

"Hi."

"Hi yourself."

"You look beautiful tonight. This dress…" He growls through a kiss.

"I figured you'd like it."

"I'll like it better when it's off."

"You always say that."

"I can't help it if my wife is the hottest thing since Mount Vesuvius."

"Nerd." I kiss him back. Since the cast and sling dictate his wardrobe for now, he's in a fitted black T-shirt with slacks—still ten-out-of-ten delectable. "They look pretty incredible, hey?"

We turn toward the dance floor where our parents are busting all sorts of moves.

"I've never seen her smile like that," Ryan says. "Did your dad come talk to you today?"

"He did. And you talked with your mom?"

"Mm-hmm."

"It seems our parents are *in lurve.*"

"Do you blame them? We are kind of awesome," he says. "Makes sense they'd be attracted to each other." Ryan slowly spins me so his back is to the crowd and I am shadowed by his height.

"I just want them to be happy. And as long as they don't break each other's hearts, holidays will be simpler with everyone gathering in one place instead of us having to split time down in Portland or whatever."

"True." He again fuses our mouths, tongue and all, before pulling back for a breath. "Any chance you wanna get out of here?"

"And what? Are you going to take me to your room? I don't know—maybe I should check with my dad first to see if he'll extend my curfew."

Ryan laughs and pushes into me, revealing that he is very much interested in breaking my curfew this evening.

"Come on, then." He hooks his pinkie around mine and I follow him out of the ballroom, my ears instantly grateful. He hums along as the Garden Gnomes fade the farther we get from the party.

We reach our front door and I open it, but Ryan stops me before I'm allowed to enter.

"Your last present awaits."

"Ryan, no . . . babe, you've done too much. *You* are enough."

"Entrez vous, madame."

I walk in, pausing only to kick off my heels, and on the kitchen island sits a huge bouquet of red roses in a sparkling crystal vase.

Propped against it is yet another red envelope that reads *OPEN ME LAST*, accompanied by a rectangular, red-wrapped box. Ryan moves in right behind me and kisses the top of my head. "Happy Valentine's Day, Hollie Porter."

I turn and stand on tiptoes to lock lips with my ravishing husband. "Thank you. I can't believe you did so much. I only bought a couple of crotchless teddies to prance around in."

A low rumble rises in his throat as he nudges his nose against mine. "Hurry up and open this, woman."

"Seriously, though, you went way overboard."

"Did not." He pecks my forehead and slides onto a barstool, nodding at the vase. "Card first, present second."

"Yes, sir." I unseal and pull another note free, only this one isn't printed in ornate calligraphy. It's in Ryan's handwriting:

> **A key made of sweetness, not brass or steel,**
> **A token of our future, both hopeful and real,**
> **It unlocks a dream, a nest for us to dwell,**
> **Beyond the Cove's charm where our love stories swell,**
> **A step to new chapters, with joy to reveal.**

I look at him, a bit confused.

"Now the box." He smiles like his team has just made the Stanley Cup Finals.

I free the flat rectangle from its red paper. Inside is a chocolate key the length of my forearm. "What is this?"

"We've been talking about maybe picking out a real house. I would never just go and buy one without you there to help choose. So, this is me, your devoted husband, sitting before you, my favorite Hollie Porter, asking if you would like to go house shopping."

"Are you serious?" I'm shaking.

"Everything's arranged with the bank. We just have to pick out what we want."

I squeal and bounce into him, throwing my arms around his neck before remembering that my knight in shining hockey gear is medically fragile. "Sorry, sorry." I kiss the back of his hand and then cup his bristled cheeks. "Can we find one with locking doors so that when our parents come to visit, we don't accidentally walk in on them?"

Ryan howls. "Yes. We will absolutely get a house with doors that lock." He runs his hand through his hair. "Speaking of our parents and awkward moments—I meant to tell you this earlier . . ."

"Oh god, what?" I move my hands from his cheeks to mine. "I don't think I can handle anything else weird."

"My mom was really worried about Acorn."

"He's fine. He passed all the silicone."

"Yeah, but, uh, she . . . offered to pay for the vet visits."

We lock eyes for a count of three.

"*Oh my god*, Ryan, that was your MOM'S vibrator?"

*The end . . . for now.*

# February 14, 1994
## Just a quick TRUE story from your author friend (that would be me)

My (then) husband arrived home from his shift and did the tired-man shuffle into a kitchen desperately in need of renovation. We'd purchased this very old house last fall, and days before moving in, folks in the area told us it was haunted. I didn't necessarily believe it, but my subconscious got hold of that whisper and ran with it. I struggled with settling in, making it feel like home. No matter how many hours I spent scrubbing and repainting and then decorating the nursery around a rubber ducky theme (everything matched—it was perfect), something wasn't *right*.

That night, my husband found me hurriedly opening windows and fanning the smoke detector, not because of any ghosts but because, for a special Valentine's Day treat, I'd attempted to make his favorite meal: chicken-fried steak.

However, I had zero idea what I was doing, and this was long before Google, so I singlehandedly transformed a halfway decent piece of beef into an inedible charred brick.

I silently begged the decades'-old smoke detector to remain quiet. Our three-month-old was *finally* dozing in her Moses basket on the kitchen table, and this was the first reprieve I'd had all day.

Valentine's Day 1994 landed on a Monday, and my husband had walked into that smoky kitchen empty-handed. I knew our budget was tight; he reminded me daily, scolded me about remembering to sort and use the coupons when I did the shopping, was furious when I secretly saved $60 to fix the gold chain of his beloved crucifix necklace he'd snagged and snapped at work. Said that saving the money behind his back showed I had the ability to sneak and keep secrets.

He'd probably be pissed that I fucked up the ten-dollar steak.

I knew better than to be disappointed about no flowers or chocolate. Me "feeling sorry for myself" would just put him in a bad mood. Doesn't mean I hadn't hoped for *something* to show he'd thought about me just once during his workday.

Surprisingly, he didn't get mad or make fun of me about the ruined meat. Just looked at it and said, "Thanks, but I'm not eating that." Followed by, he hoped I wasn't disappointed that he forgot what day it was, that he was wiped out after too many days on and not sleeping well because of the new baby. He again mentioned our tight budget (even though he earned a municipal salary and co-owned two other properties nearby). I knew we wouldn't do something as extravagant as go out for dinner, especially not when our daughter's colicky fits started around eight o'clock every night.

I scooped his wrecked dinner into the garbage and the scorched pan into the sink to soak. "Let me make you something different. I have pasta."

"Can you come sit first?" He nodded toward one of our ugly kitchen chairs. They were secondhand from some friend or family member; I'd planned on painting and recovering the seats once I could afford the supplies. I grew up with parents who never stopped renovating and renewing and remodeling; I wasn't afraid of a little sweat equity.

I sat, carefully pulling the baby's basket closer so we could gaze at her.

Well, I gazed at her.

My husband sat forward and intertwined his fingers on the

scuffed tabletop. He didn't look into the Moses basket at all. Instead, he stared right at me sitting a mere three feet away from him, and said, "I'm in love with someone else, and I need you to move out."

ॐ

It was the worst Valentine's Day ever.

But it was also the best.

Thirty years later, I'm happily married to a kind, thoughtful, artistic, supportive, hilarious GareBear. This October, we'll clink our beer mugs to celebrate twenty-four years. And that three-month-old baby girl? She's a journalist and photographer and the proud parent of Pippin Took, a miniature longhaired Dachshund who fancies himself an opera singer around dinnertime every night. Just like his mother did all those years ago.

This Valentine's Day, you may not have yet found your Ryan Fielding. Your Hollie Porter.

You may despise Valentine's Day as much as I did (for *years*).

Maybe you hate it because it's just another hyped-up, hollowed-out holiday designed to line those capitalist pockets and make everyone believe that without someone, they are no one. A flesh sack of unlovable garbage.

But your flesh sack is lovely, and you are absolutely the furthest thing from unlovable garbage, no matter how loudly the capitalists shriek that, to be a fulfilled, actualized person this (or any) Valentine's Day, you must give or receive responsibly sourced diamonds or heart-shaped boxes of Belgian chocolates or overpriced foie gras and Prosecco.

Love is out there.

Sometimes you just have to battle through the dense, suffocating fog a broken heart ushers in. You must learn to take care of yourself until the wounds seal closed and you get some distance to look back and say, "Thank fuck *that* ended."

I can't even imagine where I'd be today if Valentine's Day 1994 hadn't happened.

And I never did learn to make chicken-fried steak.

Chin up, cutie. Every single story, at its core, is about love. That includes your story too.

**XOXO,**

*Eliza*

# One more thing about cougars

...

M y beta reader (and earnest fact-checker) Katie did a deep dive on the veracity of Hollie's wildlife tidbit about how Vancouver Island has the highest concentration of cougars in the world.

**It's true.** There are an estimated 4000 cougars in British Columbia, and 600 to 800 of them live on Vancouver Island. *And they will swim to nearby islands to hunt.* If you don't believe me (or Hollie), visit:

- https://www.vancouverisawesome.com/bc-news/cougars-bc-vancouver-island-population-1946304
- https://vancouverguardian.com/vancougar-island-cougar/
- https://news.mongabay.com/2023/03/island-hopping-cougars-redraw-boundaries-of-big-cats-potential-range/
- https://www.discovervancouverisland.com/blog/cougar-swimming-story/
- https://linnet.geog.ubc.ca/efauna/Atlas/Atlas.aspx?sciname=Puma%20concolor
- https://www.inaturalist.org/guide_taxa/340264

- https://bigcatswildcats.com/cougar/
- https://www.theglobeandmail.com/canada/british-columbia/article-cougar-disquiets-small-southern-bc-island/

**For more on cougar safety:**

- https://wildsafebc.com/species/cougar
- https://www.victoriabuzz.com/2023/03/heres-what-to-do-when-you-encounter-a-cougar-on-vancouver-island/
- https://vancouverisland.com/about/facts-and-information/safety-guide-to-cougars/

It wouldn't be an Eliza Gordon project if I didn't feed you info about my favorite creatures, now, would it? Hey, nerds gotta nerd, my friend.

You're welcome.

P.S. While we're on the topic of wildlife, the big gray and black and white goose with murder in its eyes is called a **Canada goose, _not_** a Canadian goose. They also respond to **cobra chicken**. (Another hat tip to Katie for that one because I laughed for a solid ten minutes).

# Join the Raft!

Do you want to be the first to hear about new books, upcoming releases, exclusive sales, and/or life and publishing news? Then **join the raft**! I can also guarantee pictures of my very spoiled tuxedo cats and granddog, Pippin Took.

### *Sign up for Eliza's occasional, not-at-all-annoying newsletter.*

*In the wild, sea otters hold hands so they aren't separated in the tides. These groups of floating otters are called* rafts.

Welcome aboard. So glad to have you. Can you pass the Dungeness crab, please?

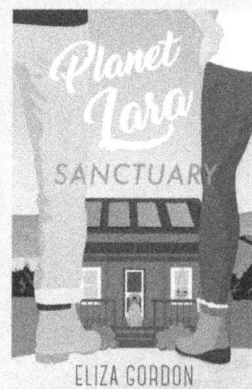

**Find the Eliza Gordon books at the following retailers in e-book, print, and audio.**

**Did you know you can ask your local library to order in Eliza's books?**

**Visit elizagordon.com for links.**

Amazon globally | Angus & Robertson | Apple Books | Audible | Audiobooks.com | Barnes & Noble | Biblioteca | Bold.de | Books-A-Million | Bookshop.org | Booktopia | Chapters/Indigo | Chirp | Everand | Google Play | Hoopla | Ingram | Kobo | Libby | Libro.fm | Mondadori | Overdrive | Powell's | Scribd | Thalia.de | 24 Symbols | Waterstones

SGA
BOOKS

www.ingramcontent.com/pod-product-compliance
Lightning Source LLC
Chambersburg PA
CBHW021132020426
42331CB00005B/741